JAMES

ABINGDON NEW TESTAMENT COMMENTARIES

JAMES

C. FREEMAN SLEEPER

Abingdon Press
Nashville

ABINGDON NEW TESTAMENT COMMENTARIES:
JAMES

Copyright 1998 by Abingdon Press

This book is printed on recycled, acid-free, elemental chlorine–free paper.

Cataloging-in-Publication data is available from the Library of Congress.

For Lee Keck
Teacher, Mentor, Scholar, Friend

CONTENTS

FOREWORD

The *Abingdon New Testament Commentaries* series provides compact, critical commentaries on the writings of the New Testament. These commentaries are written with special attention to the needs and interests of theological students, but they will also be useful for students in upper-level college or university settings, as well as for pastors and other church leaders. In addition to providing basic information about the New Testament texts and insights into their meanings, these commentaries are intended to exemplify the tasks and procedures of careful, critical biblical exegesis.

The authors who have contributed to this series come from a wide range of ecclesiastical affiliations and confessional stances. All are seasoned, respected scholars and experienced classroom teachers. They take full account of the most important current scholarship and secondary literature, but do not attempt to summarize the literature or to engage in technical academic debate. Their fundamental concern is to analyze the literary, socio-historical, theological, and ethical dimensions of the biblical texts themselves. Although all of the commentaries in this series have been written on the basis of the Greek texts, the authors do not presuppose any knowledge of the biblical languages on the part of the reader. When some awareness of a grammatical, syntactical, or philological issue is necessary for an adequate understanding of a particular text, they explain the matter clearly and concisely.

The introduction of each volume ordinarily includes subdivisions dealing with the *key issues* addressed and/or raised by the New Testament writing under consideration; its *literary genre, structure, and character*; its *occasion and situational context,* including its wider social, historical, and religious contexts; and its *theological and ethical significance* within these several contexts.

In each volume, the *commentary* is organized according to literary units rather than verse by verse. Generally, each of these units is the subject of three types of analysis. First, the *literary analysis* attends to the unit's genre, most important stylistic features, and overall structure. Second, the *exegetical analysis* considers the aim and leading ideas of the unit, deals with any especially important textual variants, and discusses the meanings of important words, phrases, and images. It also takes note of the particular historical and social situations of the writer and original readers, and of the wider cultural and religious contexts of the book as a whole. Finally, the *theological and ethical analysis* discusses the theological and ethical matters with which the unit deals or to which it points, focusing on the theological and ethical significance of the text within its original setting.

Each volume also includes a *select bibliography,* thereby providing guidance to other major commentaries and important scholarly works, and a brief *subject index.* The New Revised Standard Version of the Bible is the principal translation of reference for the series, but the authors also draw on all of the major modern English versions, and when necessary provide their own original translations of difficult terms or phrases.

The fundamental aim of this series will have been attained if readers are assisted, not only to understand more about the origins, character, and meaning of the New Testament writings, but also to enter into their own informal and critical engagement with the texts themselves.

Victor Paul Furnish
General Editor

PREFACE

Recently, just out of curiosity, I looked at the Bible that I received years ago on Children's Day (in a kind of mini-confirmation). I was startled to discover that the most heavily marked and underlined portions of that Bible were the last part of the New Testament, from Philippians through Revelation. Most of those letters and other books have continued to be near the center of my scholarly interests. My first actual presentation on James was a paper delivered at a meeting of the Society of Biblical Literature in 1990, followed in 1992 by a discussion session on James 2, which I prepared and led at the annual meeting of the Society of Christian Ethics. It was a real pleasure, then, to be invited by the editorial board of the *Abingdon New Testament Commentaries* to bring my study of James to a kind of conclusion by doing a commentary on that book.

Rex Matthews, then senior editor of academic books at Abingdon Press, was helpful to me during the preparatory stage. Professor Pheme Perkins of Boston College was the first person to read the manuscript. Her probing comments and questions helped me to see more clearly what was expected of a commentary in this series.

Because of the warm reception we had received the previous year, when I was a visiting scholar at Union Theological Seminary in Richmond, Virginia, my wife, Mamie, and I moved to Richmond in August 1996. She has been supportive of the move and of my writing, especially during the long days and evenings of 1997 while I was at the word processor.

Dr. John Trotti and the library staff at Union Seminary provided me with a carrel and with access to books and periodicals. I simply could not have completed the book by the deadline without their help and without those resources.

For five Sundays in August 1997, while I was bringing the first draft of the manuscript to a close, I was privileged to teach an adult class at Ginter Park Presbyterian Church in Richmond. My preparation for that class, combined with the perceptive comments and questions from those who attended, helped me to sharpen a number of issues. My thanks to them as well.

C. Freeman Sleeper

LIST OF ABBREVIATIONS

1 [2] Clem.	*First [Second] Clement*
1 Enoch	Ethiopic *Book of Enoch*
1QS	*Rule of the Community* (Qumran Cave 1)
AB	Anchor Bible
ANRW	*Aufstieg und Niedergang der römischen Welt*
Ant.	Josephus, *The Antiquities of the Jews*
Apoc. Abr.	*Apocalypse of Abraham*
Barn.	*Barnabas*
Bib	*Biblica*
CBQ	*Catholic Biblical Quarterly*
CNT	Commentaire du Nouveau Testament
Decal.	Philo, *On the Decalogue*
Did.	*Didache*
GNB	*The Bible in Today's English Version* (Good News Bible)
HBC	J. L. Mays, et. al. (eds.), *Harper's Bible Commentary*
Herm. Man.	Hermas, *Mandate(s)*
Hist. Eccl.	Eusebius, *The History of the Church*
HNTC	Harper's NT Commentaries
HTKNT	Herders theologischer Kommentar zum Neuen Testament
HTR	*Harvard Theological Review*
IBC	Interpretation: A Bible Commentary for Teaching and Preaching
ICC	International Critical Commentary
Int	*Interpretation*
Ira	Seneca, *On Anger* (in *Moral Essays*)
ISBE	G. W. Bromiley (ed.), *International Standard Bible Encyclopedia*

LIST OF ABBREVIATIONS

JB	*The Jerusalem Bible*
JSNTSup	Journal for the Study of the New Testament— Supplement Series
J.W.	Josephus, *The Jewish War*
LCL	Loeb Classical Library
LXX	Septuagint
MeyerC	H. A. W. Meyer, Critical and Exegetical Commentary on the New Testament
NIGTC	The New International Greek Testament Commentary
NIV	*The Holy Bible, New International Version*
NRSV	New Revised Standard Version
NTS	*New Testament Studies*
RSV	Revised Standard Version
Sir	Sirach (Ecclesiasticus; in the Apocrypha)
T. Asher	*Testament of Asher*
T. Benj.	*Testament of Benjamin*
T. Dan	*Testament of Dan*
T. Naph.	*Testament of Naphtali*
T. Jos.	*Testament of Joseph*
T. Levi	*Testament of Levi*
T Sim.	*Testament of Simeon*
WBC	Word Biblical Commentary
Wis	The Wisdom of Solomon (Apocrypha)
ZNW	*Zeitschrift für die neutestamentliche Wissenschaft*

INTRODUCTION:
READING JAMES

If you really want to understand a text, ancient or modern, an introduction is usually not the best place to begin. It is the place where a modern author presents his or her conclusions. It typically refers to other authorities, ancient and modern, whom you may not have the time or patience to read, at least not now. It presupposes that the author is an expert who has already solved all of the major problems and is now giving you the correct answers. It suggests that once you have read the introduction you will know all there is to know about the text, so that you may never have to read the text itself.

I recommend a different approach, which is more inductive and used for problem solving. According to this method, begin with your own careful reading of James. Read it all in one sitting, which should not take very long since it consists of only five relatively short chapters. Then read it several more times, each time using a different translation. If you do, you will discover several things. First, you will immediately notice differences in wording. For example, the King James Version of 1:2 speaks of "temptations"; several modern versions (RSV, NRSV, NIV, JB) speak of "trials"; J. B. Phillips covers both bases by speaking of "trials and temptations." If you have even a basic knowledge of Greek, you will want to check your Greek text to see which translation best conveys the meaning of the original text. Second, each translation has inserted bold headings to help you identify different topics. The headings are meant to give you an outline and to help you follow the flow of the book. Compare these outlines. Are they identical? If not, which ones are the most helpful? You should also raise those same questions about the outlines presented in this and other commentaries. Third, keep in mind that the present division of the text into chapters and verses was not in the original manuscripts, but was added centuries later. As you become more familiar with the text, you may want to make your own outline.

Also, as you read, look for answers to questions like the following: What topics does the author deal with? What arguments does he use to make his points? What do you notice about his language and his style? What do you learn about the author and about the people to whom he was writing? Other questions will occur to you as you read. There are no simple answers, as you will discover if you use the bibliography at the end of this book.

LITERARY ISSUES

Style

Several features of James's style are apparent even at a first reading. One is the frequent use of imperatives (at least sixty times); the clearest example is found in 4:7-10. Another obvious feature is that he addresses the audience directly as "brothers" or "my brothers," often at important transitions in the argument (e.g., 1:2; 2:1, 14; 3:1; 5:9, 12, 19). Several times the author uses rhetorical questions in which the anticipated answer is obvious. These appear especially in the central section of the book (2:1–5:6), for example in 2:4, 5, 14-16; 3:11-12. A stylistic device appears in 2:18 when an imaginary person challenges the author, although we will see in the commentary that there is some confusion about the nature and extent of that person's question. In Greek, many sentences have an introductory word or phrase like "Come now" (4:13 and 5:1) and "Listen" (5:4). Often these are glossed over in English translations, so that one purpose of a commentary is to point them out whenever they occur. There are ad hominem attacks: "you senseless person" (2:20); "adulterers" (4:4); "you double-minded" (4:8). Famous characters from the biblical tradition (Abraham, Rahab, Job, Elijah) are used as models of the kind of behavior that James wants his audience to emulate. All of these and other techniques are characteristics of a style of ancient rhetoric known as the "diatribe," which was well known in hellenistic literary circles and was particularly popular among Cynic and Stoic philosophers (Ropes 1916, 10-16; Johnson 1995b, 9-10).

Keep in mind that these rhetorical patterns were designed primarily for oral communication. Even in the case of letters, such as Paul's, they were meant to be read aloud. They were written for oral delivery by someone in the congregation, since most of the people in the audience could not read and they did not have multiple copies of the text.

Genre

In order to know how to read any piece of literature it is important to understand its genre. For example, we would not think of reading a poem as though it were a novel, or a personal letter as though it were a sermon. Unfortunately, James is not easy to classify. It has traditionally been treated as one of the General Epistles, along with Hebrews, two letters of Peter, Jude, and sometimes the three letters of John. They are called "general" because we cannot identify specific congregations or individuals to whom they were addressed. Even though 1 Peter is addressed to churches in Asia Minor, it is more of a circular letter and we learn almost nothing about local congregations.

The opening verse of James suggests that this is a letter from him to the twelve tribes in the Dispersion, without telling us where that is. However, James is obviously quite different from Paul's letters, particularly 1 Thessalonians, Galatians, and Philippians. First of all, there is no personal information about either the author or the recipients. Second, except for the salutation in 1:1, other formal characteristics of Greco-Roman correspondence seem to be missing. There is no thanksgiving, a feature that follows the salutation in all of Paul's letters except Galatians. There is no clear postscript or conclusion, which normally would consist of personal comments and perhaps a blessing or well-wishes. Therefore even scholars who accept it as a letter tend to treat it as a formal composition or an epistle. In an important article Fred Francis pointed out similarities between 1 John and James, particularly with respect to their endings. He concluded that both are indeed letters, and to support that conclusion he provided examples of ancient letters, which have a similar format. His argument has been generally accepted, but that still does not tell us very much about the content of the letter.

One suggestion (argued forcefully by Ropes) is that James is a consistent example of a diatribe, from beginning to end. However, there is no broad agreement that the diatribe is itself a genre or whether (as I have suggested above) simply a well-constructed rhetorical style.

An alternative was proposed by Martin Dibelius in his influential commentary, originally published in 1921 and revised by Heinrich Greeven in 1964. Dibelius argued that James is a collection of independent moral exhortations or parenesis. "By paraenesis we mean a text which strings together admonitions of general ethical content" (Dibelius and Greeven 1976, 3). Like wisdom literature generally, and hellenistic-Jewish wisdom in particular, such writings are addressed to a broad, anonymous audience rather than to a particular situation. As features of such literature, Dibelius mentions several characteristics: eclecticism; lack of continuity; use of catchwords to provide connections between individual units; repetition of a motif (e.g., wisdom) at various places throughout the writing; and very general admonitions or moral advice (Dibelius and Greeven 1976, 5-11). A similar piece of writing from the same general time period is known as the *Sentences of Pseudo-Phocylides*. There is no question that James contains a lot of moral exhortation, but Dibelius does not really do justice to the structure of the letter, as I will argue. As a sort of counterargument, W. W. Wessel proposed that James really consists of a series of short homilies based on the pattern of synagogue sermons, but his view has not met with a great deal of support (Wessel 1982).

A more recent proposal is that of Luke Timothy Johnson (1995b, 20-21, based on an article by E. Baasland) that James is an example of "protreptic discourse." Originally this was a speech or a tract that encouraged others to follow a particular profession and conform to its norms, more or less following the pattern of a recruiting tract. However, it could also appear as a more general call to a life of virtue, which is exactly what James represents.

Structure

Even after several close readings, James gives us the impression that these are notes, in random order, on several topics: dealing with trials in everyday living; the need for single-minded devotion to God; poverty and wealth; controlling your tongue and your temper; the role of the law as a guide to Christian living. All of this is similar to the practical advice that we find in Proverbs and especially in later Jewish wisdom literature. The same topics are dealt with several times throughout the letter, rather than being grouped together in a more logical sequence. As noted above, Dibelius argued a similar position: "in all these instances, what one finds is *paraenesis* in the form of unconnected sayings which have no real relationship to one another" (Dibelius and Greeven 1976, 3). Since verses are only loosely connected, Dibelius finds no consistent structure in the book. Individual verses may be linked by word associations, but not by any thematic development. By using the form critical method, Dibelius tried to isolate individual sayings, originally addressed to different audiences and brought together by an author with no overall plan in mind. Recent commentators (e.g., Davids, Johnson, Martin) have generally rejected that view. The presupposition of more recent work is that the author must have put the material into its present form for some reason, even though an overall pattern is not immediately apparent. In other words, recent scholars tend to be more committed to looking for a pattern, even if they cannot agree what that is (in addition to the commentaries, see Hartin 1991, 29-30 and 245-46; and Cargal 1993, 90-91, 134-36, 138-42, 170-73, 198-99). Even if we think of the book as a lot of loose beads strung together, we have to admit that the author strung them in this particular pattern rather than a different one.

After the introductory address and greeting in 1:1, there are three major sections of the book of James. Most of chapter 1 (vv. 2-27) introduces the themes to be found later. The main body (2:1–5:6) has a lot more coherence and is generally agreed to represent the greatest degree of originality on the part of the author. The concluding section (5:7-20) deals with some practical issues in the life of the church, including some that were hinted at earlier but not directly addressed.

One clue to the structure is James's use of "brothers" *(adelphoi)* as a rhetorical device to establish rapport between himself and his audience. Ordinarily he uses it as a form of direct address: "my brothers" (1:2; 2:1, 14; 3:1, 10, 12); "my beloved brothers" (1:16, 19; 2:5); and simply as "brothers" (4:11; 5:7, 9, 10, 12, 19). Only in 2:15 does he address both men and women. That verse could lead us to conclude that he intends the term to be inclusive in every case (so the NRSV translators use "brothers and sisters" or "beloved"). It could also lead to the opposite conclusion that "brothers" was addressed exclusively to the male members of the congregation except in this one case. When I have occasion to give my own translation, I will give it literally in order to convey what the text actually says. In almost every case this phrase introduces a new point or a new theme. The clearest exception is in 3:10, 12, where it concludes the argument of a section. Verse 1:16, which begins "Do not be deceived," is problematic. It is obviously used to emphasize a point, but one in the previous verses or one in the verses that follow? In the commentary we will look at arguments for each view; but in any case it functions as a transitional verse. This use of direct address, then, is a major clue to shifts in the author's argument. We should use it as a guideline unless there are compelling reasons not to do so.

In a computer age we are used to thinking in a linear fashion; we expect ideas and language to have a logical progression. James does not fit that pattern, so we need to ask whether there is some other principle of organization. In fact, there is, and it relates to shifts in themes. To return to the bead image, if you have ever strung them you know that you don't usually put all the red ones together, then the blue ones, the yellow ones, and so on. Think of James as a necklace. Each unit in chapter 1 introduces one or more themes, which are then picked up and developed in a later unit, along with new themes. In the entire book there are fewer than twenty issues. Some of these overlap and could be combined. Here is one such arrangement that lists only the major passages where themes reappear.

Unit	Theme	Also found in:
1:2-4	1. trials, temptations	1:12-16; 3:13–4:1-6; 5:13-18 (suffering)
	2. faith (also v. 6)	2:5, 14-26; 5:15
	3. endurance	5:7-11
	4. perfection/maturity	1:17; 3:2
1:5-8	5. wisdom	3:1, 13-18
	6. God as giver	1:17-18; 3:17; 4:6
	7. asking in prayer	4:2-3; 5:13-18
	8. being single-minded	3:13–4:6; 4:8
1:9-11	9. rich and poor	2:1-7, 14-17; 4:13–5:6
	10. humility	1:21; 3:16-18; 4:7-10
	11. death	1:12, 14-15; 4:13–5:10, 19-20
1:12-16	see #1, 11 above	
1:17-18	see #6 above	
	12. God's word	1:21-23; 5:10
1:19-21	13. control of speech	1:26; 2:12; 3:1-12; 4:11-12; 5:9, 12
1:22-25	14. hearing and doing	2:14-26
	15. the law	2:8-13; 4:1-6
1:26-27	see #13 above	
	16. religion as caring	2:14-17; 3:17-18; 5:13-20

The commentary itself is based on a combination of these and other clues. The units just mentioned are the basic ones in the epistle; but they can be combined into larger sections based on vocabulary, style, themes, and James's use of rhetorical devices. An outline of the book is found in the contents.

THE LETTER
IN ITS LITERARY CONTEXT

All of us are shaped by ideas and assumptions that are so ingrained that we are rarely aware of them and, even if they are challenged, we find it hard to question them. We may refer to this as our "thought world" or, to use a more contemporary term, our "symbolic universe." In this section we want to explore the thought world that frames and influences the letter of James. We can identify other documents that share his ideas and perspectives, without implying that he actually copied from them.

The Biblical Context

If we may identify four distinct moral traditions within the Old Testament (Sleeper 1992, chaps. 2–5), then it is fair to say that James appeals to all four, in various combinations. The comprehensive term is "the word of truth" (1:18) or simply "the word" (1:22-23). It is synonymous with the law, called the "perfect law" (1:25), the "law of liberty" (1:25; 2:12), and "the royal law" (2:8). In 2:8-13 the description of the law consists of only three citations: the love commandment (Lev 19:18) and the commandments against adultery and murder from the Decalogue. In 4:1-6 there are allusions to three items in the Decalogue: murder, coveting, and adultery. There is no interest, however, in the kind of detailed exegesis that we find in different forms in Qumran, in the rabbinic material, in portions of Paul's letters, and in Matthew's Gospel.

Prophetic themes are apparent in 1:27 (the definition of pure and undefiled religion as care for orphans and widows), although that theme is present in the Torah as well. A prophetic condemnation of the rich is found in 5:1-6. It is followed soon afterward by an appeal to the prophets as examples of those who endured suffering and exhibited patience while speaking in God's name. Similarly, the thought of "bringing back" to the faith those who have wandered (5:19-20) is a prophetic theme.

The wisdom theme is most prominent in 1:5-8, where it is pictured as a gift from God. It is implicit in the advice to prospective teachers in 3:1-12. It becomes the focus of James's advice in 4:13-18, where James describes the characteristics of a true wisdom that comes from above. Since there is no mention of the Holy Spirit in James, it is tempting to assume that in its place wisdom is being personified here (as it is in Prov 3:19-20 and 8:22-31 and in later

Jewish wisdom literature) as the mind of God, which guides the moral order; but James does not make such a view explicit.

Finally, there are eschatological themes throughout James in the broad sense of anticipating a reversal of this world's fortunes, particularly the relationship of the rich and the poor (e.g., 1:11; 2:13). A more apocalyptic dimension, appealing to God (or Christ) as the final judge, appears only in 4:12 and 5:9, alongside a mention of the "last days" in 5:3, a "day of slaughter" in 5:5, and "the coming of the Lord" (5:7, 8).

James rarely cites any biblical source directly, but when he does, it is always from the Septuagint (LXX) the Greek translation of the Hebrew Bible (2:8, 11, 23; 4:6; cf. 5:20). This confirms his familiarity with the Greek language.

Intertestamental Literature

The thought world closest to James is that of hellenistic-Jewish wisdom literature. By the middle of the first Christian century it had been almost four hundred years since the conquest of Alexander the Great, and during that period Palestine had been experiencing hellenizing influences almost constantly, as had Jews living in the Diaspora. Although James reflects certain ideas and phrases found in classical Greek and Roman authors, those ideas have been filtered through Jewish authors, for example in the Wisdom of Solomon and Sirach, both of which are found in the Apocrypha. Pseudepigraphal books that shed light on that thought world are the *Testament of the Twelve Patriarchs,* the *Psalms of Solomon,* and the *Sentences of Pseudo-Phocylides,* plus some passages in the apocalyptic books of *1 Enoch* and *2 Baruch.* Some of the documents found at Qumran are also helpful. The notion of the two ways of light and darkness is not mentioned in James, but his dualism of friendship with the world versus friendship with God (4:4) implies the same thought pattern. The *Rule of the Community* at Qumran (1QS) sheds light on the kind of community for which James was intended. Philo, the prolific Alexandrian-Jewish philosopher, is one of the best examples of hellenistic-Jewish thought.

The New Testament Context

Parallels between James and the synoptic Gospels, particularly the Sermon on the Mount, have long been noted (e.g., Mayor 1892, lxxxii-lxxxiv). In the past twenty years a scholarly cottage industry has developed, focused primarily on Q and the sayings in the *Gospel of Thomas*. Until very recently, however, very little attention was paid to the relationship of that material to the tradition in James (with the work of Patrick Hartin being a major exception). The following list is a conservative estimate of the contacts between James and the synoptic tradition (cf. also Mussner 1964, 48-50; and Davids 1982, 47-48).

James	Q parallels	Topic
1:5-6	Matt 7:7-8 = Luke 11:9-10	asking in faith
1:5, 17	Matt 7:11 = Luke 11:13	God as gracious giver
2:5	Matt 5:3 (cf. v. 5) = Luke 6:20	heirs of the kingdom
2:10	Matt 5:18-19 = Luke 16:17	keeping the whole law
2:13	Matt 5:7; cf. Luke 6:36	on judging
3:12	Matt 7:16-18 = Luke 6:43-44	bearing good fruit
4:2*b*-3	Matt 7:7-8 = Luke 11:9-10	asking and receiving
4:4	Matt 6:24 = Luke 13:13	friendship with God; on not having two masters
4:10	Matt 23:12 = Luke 14:11; 18:14	humility before God
4:11	Matt 7:1-2 = Luke 6:37-38	on not judging
5:2-3	Matt 6:19-21 = Luke 12:33-34	no treasure on earth
5:19-20	Matt 18:15 = Luke 17:3	on bringing back a sinner

James	Other Parallels	Topic
2:11	Matt 5:21-30	saying against adultery
2:15-16	Matt 25:31-46	care for the poor as a basis for God's judgment
3:18	Matt 5:9	on being peacemakers
4:8	Matt 5:8	on being pure in heart
5:12	Matt 5:34-37	on not taking oaths
1:5-6	Mark 11:23-24	on praying without doubting
2:8	Mark 12:28-34	"love your neighbor as yourself"
4:9	Luke 6:25	laugh/mourn/weep
5:1	Luke 6:24	woes on the rich
5:17	Luke 4:25	Elijah and the drought

At least three things are worth noting about these sayings in the letter. First, they are not presented as sayings of Jesus; James never claims Jesus' authority for any of these words! Rather, they have become part of the wisdom tradition that James is passing on. From a literary point of view, they have become the words of the author himself. Second, unlike the synoptic Gospels, James never puts these sayings in a narrative setting. The letter genre dictates the way in which the sayings are presented. Third, the parallels are striking enough so that James must become part of future discussions about Q and the tradition of Jesus' sayings. There is no indication that James was familiar with the synoptic Gospels in their final form. Therefore these sayings represent an early tradition, whether or not the brother of the Lord was its transmitter.

Is there any connection between James and the letters of Paul? None that is detectable. Obviously some words and phrases appear in both sources, but they tend to be part of the broader Christian tradition and do not indicate that either author knew the work of the other. Detailed issues will be dealt with in the commentary on 2:14-26, but we may anticipate some of the conclusions. First, we must resist Luther's view that James is defective when measured against Paul's Christology and his view of justification (especially in Gal 2–4 and Rom 1–4). Second, if the author of James did know anything about Paul's theology it was secondhand and inaccurate;

he did not learn it from reading Paul's letters. Paul never claimed that a person is justified "by faith alone" (see Jas 2:24), and he certainly expected believers to show the fruits of their faith. Moreover, James seems to know nothing about Paul's rejection of "works of the law" as a basis for being justified in God's sight. The two authors are simply dealing with different issues. Third, the debate is not about faith versus works; neither author would have accepted that formulation. If that is what James understood Paul to be saying, then he misunderstood Paul. As we shall see, the dating of James depends in part on how we explain his relation to Paul. (Out of a long list of authors who have dealt with this topic, see especially Dan Via.)

When we turn to 1 Peter there are an unusual number of parallels. J. B. Mayor (1892, xcv-ci) thought any unbiased reader would conclude that the author of that letter had borrowed from James. Some scholars have thought the direction of borrowing ought to be reversed (e.g., Selwyn, Reicke). In recent scholarship the prevailing opinion is that they are both dealing with a "common stock of ethical teaching" (Laws 1980, 20). Therefore, let us reexamine the evidence.

There does seem to be a common core, although it is not extensive enough to include James either as part of a baptismal catechism or as part of a persecution formula (Selwyn 1958, 384-466, based in part on the work of Philip Carrington). The core consists of at least three Old Testament quotations, which each writer interprets in different ways. First, in 1:10-11 James offers a paraphrase of Isa 40:6-7 about the grass withering and the flower fading. First Peter 1:24-25a cites the whole passage, but in the context of a new birth through "the living and enduring word of God" (v. 23). Thus it is likely that Jas 1:18, "[God] gave us birth by the word of truth," is an extension of 1:10-11. The second passage is Prov 3:34, which comes at a critical position when James shifts to a discussion of virtues (4:6; see commentary). In 1 Pet 5:5 it occurs in the context of a long passage about suffering, but, as in James, the emphasis is on being humble (Jas 4:10; 1 Pet 5:5, 6). Third, the letter of James ends at 5:20 by saying that whoever brings back a sinner "will cover a multitude of sins," an allusion to Prov 10:12. In this case, 1 Pet 4:8 quotes the saying in exactly the same form as James, except the subject is love. There is an echo of 1 Pet 4:8 in *1 Clem.* 49:5, although with a slight change in wording. In all of these instances, Peter is more interested in exegeting the text and applying it to the current situation of his audience.

Two other passages are often considered to belong to this core. One is the opening salutation "To the twelve tribes in/of the Dispersion." Since this form of address is unique in the New Testament, it is hard to see how it could be part of a general collection of moral recommendations. A simpler solution is that the author of 1 Peter borrowed it and adapted it to a new situation (see commentary). This applies to the other passage as well (Jas 1:2-3 = 1 Pet 1:6-7). There is a common emphasis on rejoicing in trials and on a faith that endures and grows. However, the differences in 1 Peter are striking: the insertion of a typical blessing or thanksgiving after the salutation (1:3-5); and an eschatological orientation (1:7). Both passages appear at the beginning of the letters, and they share the same general theme of enduring trials; but it is difficult to see what the wording of an earlier "core" would have been. It is easier to see how the author of 1 Peter took the opening of James and expanded it.

What the thesis of a common tradition does not easily explain is the large number of verbal and thematic parallels between these two letters, particularly words that are seldom found elsewhere in the New Testament. There are at least twenty of these, so there is room to give only a sample. Others will be dealt with in the commentary.

James		Comparison with 1 Peter
1:12:	"the **crown** of life"	5:4 "crown of glory"
1:21:	"**Therefore rid yourselves** of . . . **wickedness**"	*(kakia* here and in 2:1, but translated as "malice" in the NRSV)
1:25:	"**look**"	1:12; cf. only Luke 24:12 and John 20:5
1:27:	"**undefiled**"	1:4; cf. only Heb 7:26; 13:4
1:27:	"**unstained**"	1:19; cf only 1 Tim 6:14 and 2 Pet 3:14

2:1:	"favoritism"	as a verb in 2:9 (NRSV: "show partiality"); 1:17 (with a negative prefix; NRSV: "impartially"); cf. only Rom 2:11; Eph 6:9; Col 3:25
2:5:	"heirs"	1:4 (inheritance)
3:13:	"your good **life**"	1:15, 18; 2:12; 3:1, 2, 16 (usually translated "conduct" in the NRSV; only six other occurrences)
3:17:	"without . . . hypocrisy"	1:22 (where the same word is translated "genuine" in the NRSV and "sincere" in the RSV); cf. only Rom 12:9; 2 Cor 6:6; 1 Tim 1:5; 2 Tim 1:5
4:1:	"at war"	2:11; only four other occurrences
5:19:	"if anyone **wanders** and is **brought back**"	2:25

These parallels do not, of course, establish literary dependence in anything like our modern sense, which practically involves plagiarism. However, they do suggest that the author of 1 Peter was familiar with James, for three reasons: the difficulty of establishing what a "common tradition" might have looked like, apart from the three Scripture quotations; the striking similarity in the salutations and opening statements; and the sharing of an unusual vocabulary. Regardless of your decision on the issue of "familiarity," two things remain true. One is that the vocabulary of both of these letters has a great deal in common with those New Testament writings generally considered to be from the last third of the first Christian century (Ephesians, the Pastorals, Hebrews), so that an extremely late date for James is unlikely. Second, 1 Peter uses the parallel material in a very different way and with quite different emphases.

The Later Christian Tradition

When we look at Christian literature produced near or after the end of the first century, we find a strange pattern. Second Peter, which is included in the canon, is often dated well into the next century. Other writings that are not included in the canon may be considerably earlier. For example, the *Didache* or "the teaching of the Twelve Apostles" is a manual for the life of a community that was probably Jewish Christian in origin. It contains material that is similar to James and to Matthew. It is difficult to date the document with any precision, but almost certainly it was written no later than the early part of the second century CE. The theme of the "two ways" of life and death that dominates the document is similar in thought, if not in language, to James's contrast between friendship with God and friendship with the world. *First Clement,* sent from the church at Rome to the church in Corinth, and named for the bishop of Rome who served toward the end of the first century, is generally assumed to have been written at about that same time. It bears some striking resemblances to both James and 1 Peter. In some passages such as Jas 4:8 (see commentary), the parallels are so striking that we may assume that Clement was actually commenting on that verse or passage in James. If so, that letter and 1 Peter would be two of the earliest pieces of evidence for the existence of the letter of James. An even more convincing source for the influence of James in the church, probably in the early part of the second century, is *The Shepherd of Hermas,* especially the section known as the *Mandate(s).* It develops James's warning against being "double-minded," along with other themes such as the role of poverty, the misuse of speech, and endurance (Johnson 1995b, 75-79).

Among the many documents discovered at Nag Hammadi in Egypt in 1945 are apocryphal works attributed to James. They most likely originated in Syria and show the influence of Gnostic thought in varying degrees. In the *Apocryphon of James,* the Risen Christ speaks to him and Peter. In the *First Apocalypse of James,* Christ speaks to James alone, addressing him as "my brother" and foretelling his sufferings. The *Second Apocalypse of James* then describes his martyrdom.

One of the puzzles about the letter is why it took so long for it to be accepted into the canon. The earliest traditions about the person of James, which we will examine later, date from the latter half of the second century. About the same time, the letter was accepted as authentic by Origen, who probably learned about it in Caesarea. The first complete texts of the letter that are available to us were written in Alexandria during the late-third to fifth centuries, although there are some earlier partial texts. These form the basis of the text used in this study, the twenty-seventh edition of the Nestle-Aland critical edition of the Greek New Testament. There are relatively few textual issues, and they will be discussed in the commentary. James was treated as canonical in the East by the beginning of the third century, presumably because of its Palestinian origin and the popularity of James in Egypt (e.g., in the Nag Hammadi texts already mentioned). However, it took nearly another century before it was accepted in the West by Jerome (with qualifications) and Augustine. There are, no doubt, several reasons for the long delay. One was legitimate doubts about its authorship, especially since James was not an "apostle" in the technical sense. Another was the gradual disappearance of the "Jewish Christianity," which the letter seems to represent. Perhaps most important was the identification of the figure of James with the growing Gnostic movement represented in the Nag Hammadi texts. Clement of Alexandria, in one of the oldest references to the death of James (see below), expressed reservations on just this point. Despite the long delay in gaining official recognition, if there are indeed allusions to James in 1 Peter, *1 Clement*, and *Hermas, Mandate(s)*, then there is evidence that the text existed before the end of the first century.

THE LETTER
IN ITS SOCIAL CONTEXT

The Audience

Who were the recipients of this letter? Because of the genre of the letter and its very general moral teaching, there are no personal details about the recipients. Theoretically, it should be possible to learn something about the real audience from the implied readers; but in this case it is not really possible to do that.

The salutation is to the "twelve tribes in the Dispersion" (1:1). Especially from the time of the Babylonian exile in the sixth century BCE, large numbers of Jews were forced to live outside the promised land. By the first century CE there were Jewish communities in all of the major cities of the Roman Empire: Rome, Alexandria, Antioch, Ephesus, Corinth. Collectively, they were referred to as Jews of the Dispersion or Diaspora (i.e., those who were "scattered"). One eschatological hope was that God would eventually gather all of the tribes and reunite them in the Holy Land (e.g., Zech 10). James's use of the phrase raises at least two important questions.

First, who was he addressing? Largely on the basis of this passage, some scholars have argued that James was originally a Jewish document that was later given a Christian veneer by adding christological titles in 1:1 and 2:1. That view has not been widely accepted, for reasons that I hope to make clear in the commentary. A second view, at the other end of the spectrum, is that the phrase is meant metaphorically to refer to all Christians. Thus it assumes that James was written at a later date, when the distinction between Jewish and Gentile Christians no longer existed. The phrase is used that way in 1 Pet 1:1. A middle position, and I think the most likely one, is that the intended recipients were Jewish Christians living outside Judea. That is about all we can conclude from his address to them.

For those writers who see "the historical James" as the author of the letter, either in its present form or in an earlier version, Acts 11:19-26 provides a likely historical setting. "Now those who were scattered [the same Greek stem as Diaspora] because of the persecution that took place over Stephen traveled as far as Phoenicia, Cyprus, and Antioch, and they spoke the word to no one except Jews" (v. 19). That passage goes on to say that in Antioch some men began to speak to Greeks as well, and it was there that disciples were first called "Christians." Acts later reports that after James had become head of the church in Jerusalem, he had contact with Christians in Antioch, both by letter (Acts 15:22-29; cf. 21:25) and by a delegation claiming to speak for him (Gal 2:12). That letter dealt with quite different issues, particularly ritual practices, which do not appear at all in James. It is debatable whether that letter originated with James or whether it was Luke's reconstruction. In any case, the few linguistic parallels between that letter and the letter of James fall far short of demonstrating that the same person was the author of both. About all we can glean from Acts is the impression that James was in contact with Christians who had been "scattered." That would lend credibility to a letter sent out under his name, even at a later date.

Leaving Acts aside, the letter of James itself contains so many affinities with Q and Matthew that it still belongs within the tradition of Jewish Christianity. In other words, even if James is only the putative and not the actual author of the letter that bears his name, we can conclude that the recipients were Jewish Christians who were familiar with the Greco-Roman moral tradition: its topics, its modes of argumentation, and its illustrations.

Second, where were they located? Despite the links between Q sayings and James, the communities pictured in those two documents are not necessarily located in the same place. Moreover, even if it could be proven that Q originated in Galilee among some of Jesus' earliest followers, it is hard to believe that Christians living in Jesus' own homeland would be addressed as belonging to the "twelve tribes in the Dispersion." A more likely setting is western Syria, probably Antioch, for reasons mentioned above (the link between earliest congregations in Jerusalem and Christians in Antioch). The mention of early and late rains in 5:7 would apply to that area (see the commentary), as well as to Galilee. Of course, that still does not enable us to determine whether this was an authentic letter from James to Christians in Antioch or (more likely) a letter composed there in his name and intended for Jewish Christians in other cities, particularly Alexandria.

James does presuppose a few other things about his audience, most of which will be discussed in more detail in the commentary. For example, they were facing trials of some sort (1:2). The trials might include the treatment they have received at the hands of the rich: lawsuits (2:6-7); economic deprivation (5:4); and possibly the murder of some of their leading members (5:6). However, these are meant to be illustrative, and none of them can be traced to a specific geographical location. Nothing in the letter suggests any kind of persecution, or even harassment, as severe as that described in 1 Peter. It does appear that at least the majority of the recipients were poor. References to agriculture in 5:4, 7 suggest that many of them knew about farming from personal experience, even if they themselves were not farmers. Similarly, the references to ships (1:6; 3:4-5) implies that they knew something about sailing, even if they were not sailors. We know that there were various kinds of conflict within the community (e.g., 4:1-4) but the rhetoric does not allow us to reconstruct the crime scene in any detail.

There has been a long debate about the role of poverty in early Christianity. One position has been that a communal sharing of goods was an entrance requirement. According to 1QS, persons who wanted to attain full membership in the Qumran community had to designate all of their personal goods to be communal property. Acts suggests that there was a similar requirement in the first Christian community in Jerusalem (2:43-47; 4:32-37) and that "the poor" was a self-designation for its members (see Keck and Kelly for a refutation of these arguments). A full discussion of this issue would have to include the so-called "communism" of the Jerusalem church and Paul's "collection" for the poor among the saints (Rom 15:26; Gal 2:10). Suffice it to say that neither in Acts nor in Paul's seven letters generally considered to be genuine nor in James is poverty considered either a virtue or a requirement for becoming a Christian. An alternative view, which finds support in James, is that "the poor" accurately describes the social situation of most early Christians. It is reflected in Luke's version of the first beatitude ("Blessed are you who are poor," Luke 6:20). A third interpretation, which is compatible with either of the other positions, is that the first Christians understood their poverty in light of Old Testament passages that lament the situation of the poor and oppressed, together with passages that anticipate God's reversal of fortunes and the restoration of the poor (e.g., Isa 41:17; Pss 10:12, 17-18; 37:1-22; 86:1; Prov 16:19; for a detailed discussion see Pleins 1992, 408-13). It is reflected in Matthew's version of the same beatitude ("Blessed are the poor in spirit," Matt 5:3). In any case, it is no wonder that James has proven attractive to liberation theologians (e.g., Tamez, Hanks). However, as already noted, nothing in James suggests that poverty in itself was a virtue, even though wealth was seen to be seductive (2:1-4; 4:13–5:6) and perhaps even demonic (3:13).

The similarity between Q and James is not limited to the words of Jesus. Richard Horsley (1989a, 106-29) has suggested a "provisional sketch" of the community that preserved the Q sayings, located in Galilee. Many of the characteristics of that community are strikingly similar to the audience pictured in James. In both cases, most of the members were poor. They expected a renewal of the social order or a reversal of their social status. They were encouraged to care for one another (reciprocity), particularly for the poor among them. They experienced healings and exorcisms, although exorcisms are not mentioned in James. Two other items in Q are not present in James. The first is that the community had developed procedures for resolving disputes; James encourages them to do so, but no such procedures are mentioned. The other is that in Q there is a new, egalitarian view of "family," an issue that is not directly mentioned anywhere in James. If the sketch given by Horsley is accurate, then it suggests that the Jesus-movement produced communities in more than one location that had very similar lifestyles.

The Jewish character of the Jacobean community is reinforced by the reference to their place of meeting as an assembly (Gk.: "synagogue" [2:2]); only in 5:14 are they referred to as a "church" (Gk.: *ekklēsia*). There is no mention of any church officials other than teachers (3:1) and elders (5:14), which strongly suggests a pattern drawn from the Jewish tradition. At the same time, there is no mention of the temple or Pharisaic ritual requirements, nor is there any suggestion of new patterns of worship that might have developed. Instead, the focus is on the building of character and on the moral life.

THE LETTER:
AUTHORSHIP AND DATING

James the Person

The internal evidence—that is, information found in the letter itself—says simply that James is a servant of Jesus Christ (1:1). He makes no claim to be one of the twelve who formed Jesus' inner circle, and in fact he is never listed as one of them. Also, in contrast to Paul, he never claims to be an apostle. In fact, the only other piece of information about him is that he is a teacher; note "all of us" in 3:2, referring back to his mention of teachers in 3:1. If the letter in its present form was written after his death as a tribute to him, then it is possible that the term "the righteous one" (5:6, 16) would have been understood as a reference to him.

Within the New Testament there are several unlikely candidates for the authorship of the letter. One does appear in the list of the twelve, James son of Alphaeus (Matt 10:3 = Mark 3:18 = Luke 6:15; Acts 1:13). We know nothing else about him, nor about James called "the younger" (Mark 15:40), the son of a Mary and a brother of Joseph (Matt 27:56) or Joses (Mark 15:40). This is apparently the same Mary who appears at the empty tomb in Mark 16:1 and Luke 24:10, and who is called "the other Mary" in Matt 28:1. Another James, the father of a Judas (not Iscariot) is mentioned twice by Luke (Luke 6:16 and Acts 1:13), but otherwise both the father and the son remain anonymous. The duplication of names (James, Judas, Jude, Mary) can only lead to the conclusion that there was a considerable degree of confusion in the early tradition. The only person with enough stature to be considered a candidate is James, son of Zebedee, usually paired with his brother John as one of the twelve (Matt 10:2 = Mark 3:17 = Luke 6:14; cf. Acts 1:13). He was a fisherman (Matt 4:21-22 = Mark 1:19-20; cf. Luke 5:10). During Jesus' ministry he seems to have played an active role as part of an "inner circle" within the twelve: at the healing of Jairus's daughter (Mark 5:37 = Luke 8:51); at the Transfiguration (Matt 17:1 = Mark 9:2 = Luke 9:28); at a village of the Samaritans (Luke 9:51-56); at the Mount of Olives (Mark 13:3); and at Gethsemane (Matt 26:37 = Mark 14:33). He was a leader in the early church (linked wit.h Peter in Acts 3:1, 3, 11; 4:1-31; 8:25). Two things rule him out. Luke calls Peter and John (and therefore presumably James as well) "uneducated and ordinary men" (Acts 4:13); and he was martyred in 42 CE (Acts 12:1-2), much too early to have written such a complex letter.

The likely candidate is called a brother of Jesus in the gospel tradition, along with Judas and Joses (Joseph) and Simon (Matt

13:55 = Mark 6:3). However, Mark reports that Jesus' family tried to rescue him from a crowd that thought he was out of his mind (Mark 3:19*b*-21) and that Jesus, in effect, separated himself from his immediate family (Mark 3:31-35). John's Gospel is even more negative about the attitude that his brothers had toward him (John 7:3-5). There is no evidence that James or the others identified as brothers played any positive role during Jesus' ministry in Galilee. For that reason, scholars who claim that James's letter contains words that he heard directly from Jesus' own mouth are being piously sentimental. But that brings into sharper focus the question of how James became not only a disciple but a prominent leader of the "mother church" in Jerusalem.

The best answer is found in 1 Cor 15. Paul refers to a pre-Pauline tradition (vv. 3-5), which records the earliest resurrection appearances. Apparently Paul then expanded the original list of appearances (vv. 5-6), including one to James alone (v. 7). In the absence of any better explanation, that event may have been the turning point in James's life and his career. In another context Paul mentions that Jesus' brothers were missionaries and were married (1 Cor 9:5), but it is not clear whether that information included James.

According to Acts 12:17, soon after the death of James the son of Zebedee and just after his own miraculous release from prison, Peter gives the command "Tell this to James and to the believers." Nothing in Acts, or anywhere else, explains how Jesus' brother had come to assume a leadership role. His identity and his role is confirmed from a variety of sources. One important source is Paul, who says that on his first trip to Jerusalem after becoming a Christian, he met with only two people. One was Cephas (Peter), with whom he spent fifteen days. Then Paul claims "I did not see any other apostle except James the Lord's brother" (Gal 1:19). That is important because he explicitly identifies James as "the Lord's brother," thus confirming Acts 12:17. The phrase "any other apostle" is more controversial. It can mean that Paul saw no other apostle (except Cephas), but he did see James; or it can mean that he considered James as another apostle. The latter is less likely, since in 1 Cor 9:5 he distinguishes the apostles from "the brothers of the

Lord." In either case, we have to remember that Paul has a broader concept of an apostle than we find in Acts.

Both Gal 2:1-10 and Acts 15:1-21 contain reports of a meeting held in Jerusalem, probably in the year 48 or 49 CE. The relationship of the two accounts is one of the thorniest issues in New Testament studies. Both accounts agree that the purpose of the meeting was to decide whether or not Gentiles would be required to convert to Judaism in order to become Christians. Both accounts agree that James played a decisive role and that the position of Paul and Barnabas concerning the Gentile mission was approved. However, Luke (in contrast to Paul's account) tells us that a letter was sent to Antioch, stipulating four minimal ritual requirements for Gentile converts (Acts 15:23-29; 21:25); James is often considered to have been the author of that letter. Some scholars point to verbal similarities between this letter and James as proof that both came from the same author. However, that is a circular argument: James wrote the letter in Acts, so he must have written the canonical letter as well; and the fact that he wrote the canonical letter confirms the portrait of James in Acts 15. The argument presupposes that Luke, writing at least a generation later, gave a verbatim report of what James said at that meeting and of what he wrote in a letter produced as a result of the meeting. Paul also reports a later conflict in Antioch, which he blames on representatives from James (Gal 2:11-12), over the issue of table fellowship between Jewish and Gentile Christians. From the evidence we have, that issue was not discussed in Jerusalem, or at least it was not settled there. It is not clear exactly what the position of James was on that issue, and whether he had actually sent those delegates to Antioch. Implicit in the reports by both Paul and Luke is the fact that James held a key leadership position that applied not only to Jerusalem but also to Antioch and to the newly opening Gentile mission field.

Acts 21:17-26 describes the last contact between Paul and James. It basically confirms Paul's position that the letter to Antioch was not approved at the conference in Jerusalem but was sent later without his knowledge. It did not apply to all of the Gentile churches that Paul had established. Acts also shows Paul as willing to undergo a rite of purification, along with four other men, in order to mollify the strict Jewish community in Jerusalem.

The only other New Testament reference to James occurs in Jude 1, where the author refers to himself as "Jude, a servant of Jesus Christ and brother of James" (see Bauckham).

The later tradition confirms, adds to, and embellishes the picture of James that we have already established. One of the most important pieces of new information comes from the Jewish historian Josephus (*Ant.* 2.200). He reports that in 62 CE James, along with some others, was killed at the initiative of the high priest Ananus during a brief break in the succession of Roman procurators. James, identified by Josephus as "the brother of Jesus who was called the Christ," was condemned by the Sanhedrin for violating the law and was stoned to death.

The church historian Eusebius, in his *Ecclesiastical History* in the early part of the fourth century, reports two earlier traditions. Both apparently derive from the latter half to the end of the second century. According to Hegesippus, James was the leader of the church in Jerusalem and was regarded as "the Just" (or "Righteous one"). The impression is that James was accepted by Jewish leaders because he prayed in the temple for the salvation of Israel and wore linen clothes like a priest. In fact, he prayed so much that his knees were like those of a camel. This portrait suggests that James was an ascetic. It concludes by saying that he was thrown from the temple, but he did not die until he was stoned and beaten to death with a club. According to Clement of Alexandria, James was idolized as "the Just (Righteous)" and as a true example of a person who suffered persecution bravely, a theme seen already in Jas 5:7-11. This account also reports that he was thrown down from the pinnacle of the temple. Eusebius himself adds that James was considered the first bishop of the church in Jerusalem. In the Nag Hammadi documents, which apparently originated in Syria but became part of the Gnostic tradition within the Coptic church in Egypt, James is consistently described as "the Just." The tradition that he was thrown from the temple and then beaten and stoned is reported in the *Second Apocalypse of James* (61). One of the pericopes in the *Gospel of*

Thomas quotes Jesus as saying "Wherever you are, you are to go to James the righteous, for whose sake heaven and earth came into being" (12).

Unfortunately, these traditions are not very reliable. The most obvious conclusion is that ". . . James was variously appropriated by diverse groups who fitted his figure to their own purposes. In these traditions, James is much more a fictional than a historical character" (Johnson 1995b, 99).

The Authorship and Dating of the Letter

The two questions "Who actually wrote the letter?" and "When?" are interdependent. If James was not the author, then speculation about the dating has sometimes moved well into the second century. However, there are serious objections to such a late date. The farther removed this anonymous author was from the death of James and the effective demise of Jewish Christianity, the less reason there would be to write a letter in his name. Also, by that time, the figure of James had become identified with the Gnostic fringe of the church. In addition, there is growing evidence (cited above) that James was known and used by Christian writers around the end of the first century, which sets an upper limit on the date of composition.

If, however, James actually wrote the letter, then there are two possibilities. The earliest possible date would be prior to the conference in Jerusalem, that is, before 48 CE. This would explain why James misunderstood Paul's view of righteousness based on faith apart from the law, since Paul did not formulate his view in those terms until his letters to the Galatians and the Romans several years later. It would also explain the failure of James to mention a Gentile mission. On the other hand, the absence in the letter of any concern for ritual runs counter to the letter in Acts 15, and the failure to mention the temple contradicts the image of James in the later Christian tradition, as we have seen. The really decisive argument against the early date is the use of such fluent Greek at such an early stage in James's career.

If James was the author, another possibility is that the letter was written in the early 60s, just prior to his death. Because of his position in the Jerusalem church, it is certainly possible that his Greek would be fluent enough to write the letter. Ralph Martin makes a strong case for the fact that an original core derives from James, "whether as a collection of 'sayings of James the Just' or some specimen homilies that he gave in his capacity as titular head of the Jerusalem *Urgemeinde* or 'mother church' " (Martin 1988, 221). This collection was later edited and polished. Unfortunately, this thesis requires two locations for the composition of the letter (a first one in Jerusalem, a second one in Antioch); two dates (one in the early 60s, another a generation or so later); and two writers (James as the original author, and a later anonymous editor). Martin offers no criteria for distinguishing early from late material but suggests that the editor added the salutation in 1:1, an attack on a distorted Paulinism, and the final exhortation in 5:19-20 (96, 221). Pheme Perkins's critique is on target: "Martin's secondary setting, the reworking of James's original text by a Hellenistic Jewish editor in Antioch, provides a more likely account of the origin of the letter as a whole" (Perkins 1995, 84).

If the references to "the righteous (or "just") one" in 5:6, 16 are allusions to James, then the letter was written after James's death and after the destruction of Jerusalem, therefore after 70 CE. However, it seems to be earlier than Matthew, since the author does not seem to be aware of some of the latest editorial material in that Gospel (e.g., Hartin 1991, 241-43). Also, as I have argued above, James was known to Christian writers at the end of the first century. Thus it was probably written in the decade between the mid-70s and the mid-80s.

The name of James serves two functions. First, it points to the early (probably oral) tradition of Jesus' sayings preserved in the letter, which is an alternative to the Q tradition. The "historical James" may in fact be the person who preserved some or all of those sayings in an earlier form, but that is doubtful since Jesus is never cited as the source of the sayings. Second, the choice of his name honors the memory of one of the great architects of the early church, the "righteous one," whose contributions were in danger of being lost as Jewish Christianity was beginning to disappear. Indeed, the main purpose of this letter is to preserve that tradition of hellenistic-Jewish Christianity.

THEMES IN THE LETTER

Regardless of authorship, we can look at the major themes in the letter as a reflection of a hellenized Jewish Christianity.

Theological Issues

Despite the claim of Dibelius (Dibelius and Greeven 1976, 21, 48) that James has no theology, there is a lot of raw material in the letter. To take an obvious case, James uses "the Lord" fourteen times. In most cases it follows the Old Testament pattern by referring to God (1:7; 4:14; 5:10, 11 [twice], 15). That is especially clear when it is qualified as "the Lord and Father" (3:9) and "the Lord of hosts" (5:4). On the other hand, the title has been transferred to Christ in 1:1 and 2:1, and probably in 5:7, 8 as well, since "the coming of the Lord" in early Christianity usually referred to the return of Christ. In two cases (4:10 and 5:14) the reference is ambiguous, but probably refers to God.

Additional attributes of God are that God is a generous giver (1:5, 17) who is beyond temptation (1:13). God is the "Father of lights" (1:17) who is righteous (1:20). God is one (2:19) and the source of wisdom (3:17). God "opposes the proud, but gives grace to the humble" (4:6). God is the one lawgiver and judge (4:12) who will raise up those who pray for healing (5:15). In all of these passages there is nothing that should surprise us, given the literary context that we have examined.

It is true that James says very little about Jesus Christ except that he is Lord, which was an extraordinary claim to be made by early Jewish Christians. We learn only slightly less about Jesus' earthly life from James than we do from Paul. On the other hand, Paul's concentration on the death and resurrection of Christ is completely missing, as Luther correctly observed. There is no mention of the Holy Spirit, although Wisdom peforms some of the same functions that the Spirit does in other New Testament writings (Davids 1982,

53-56), even though wisdom is not personified as it is in Proverbs (3:19-20; 8:22-31) and in Sirach (1:1-21; 15:1-10; 24:1-22).

As elsewhere in the wisdom tradition, the focus of this letter is on practical wisdom. It offers guidance for everyday living, not just for individuals but for the community as a whole.

Anthropological Issues

There is no single view of human nature in this letter. For example, 1:14-16 presents a rather modern view that sin is a product of our own desires. Unless its growth is checked, it leads inevitably to death. Similarly, in 4:1-2 conflicts and disputes within the community are the result of internal cravings and desires that have not been resolved. James is describing "divided selves" as the source of public violence.

On the other hand, 2:19 recognizes the existence of demonic powers, but stops short of saying that they are the cause of human sin. In 3:14-15, conflict seems to be the result of both inner emotions ("bitter envy and selfish ambition") and a wisdom that is "earthly, unspiritual, devilish." This suggests that sin is more than personal failure; it is also the result of external forces. The idea that people are driven by conflicting impulses, one divine and the other demonic, appears in Jewish thought at approximately the same time when James was composed. It appears in Qumran, especially in 1QS 4, and in later rabbinic literature.

James never suggests that these external forces relieve people of personal responsibility. Instead, the recommended course of action is to submit to God and resist the devil (4:7).

Ethical Issues

According to James, the moral life flows from this view of human nature. It ultimately involves a decision of whether or not to devote yourself totally to God and become a friend of God (4:4). Christians are "those who love [God]" (1:12; 2:5). To do that means to develop character. William Brown, in his book and in personal conversation, was the first person to introduce me to the role that character plays in wisdom literature, including James (Brown 1996,

160-64). That theme explains the need in our personal lives to grow in endurance toward maturity (1:2-4), to endure temptation (1:12), to control our speech and our anger (1:19-21, 26), and to be doers of the word (1:22-25). All of these themes are found in the opening chapter, and as noted earlier they are developed throughout the letter. It also explains the focus on cultivating virtues, particularly in 3:17-18 and 4:7-10.

This emphasis on character applies not just to individuals, but to the community as a whole. That is why James emphasizes concern for one another, particularly the poor (1:27; 2:14-17) and the sick (5:13-20) and those who have wandered away (5:19-20). That is why members of the community should not speak ill of one another (3:9-10; 4:11-12) or take any oaths (5:12). Instead, the expression of a wisdom from above is to create peace (3:17-18).

The alternative to loving God is to be "double-minded" (1:8; 4:8). That is equivalent to being a friend of the world (4:4). It means having a worldly wisdom that is marked by envy, selfishness, hypocrisy, and partiality rather than cooperation (3:15-17). James warns outsiders against pursuing wealth for its own sake, since that leads to arrogance and boasting (4:13-17); and presumably that warning applies to Christians as well.

A summary of James's moral advice can be found in 1:21: "Therefore rid yourselves of all sordidness and rank growth of wickedness, and welcome with meekness the implanted word that has the power to save your souls."

COMMENTARY

SALUTATION (1:1)

The letter opens with a salutation typical of ancient letters. It identifies the sender as James (*Iakōbos* in Greek, so that the adjectival form in English is Jacobean) and the recipients as "the twelve tribes in the Dispersion." It then adds the simple "greetings" (*chairein*, an infinitive form of the Greek word meaning "rejoice"). Many other New Testament letters have a more elaborate greeting: "grace and peace" or "grace, mercy, and peace." In most of Paul's letters, this salutation is followed by a thanksgiving, the body of the letter, exhortation, personal greetings, and a benediction. Except for the body, those other features are missing in James, but nevertheless it is a real letter, the purpose of which is to instruct the recipients about Christian moral character.

◊ ◊ ◊ ◊

Despite the information contained in this verse, what do we really learn about the author and his audience? He tells us nothing about himself except that he is a servant or slave *(doulos)* of both God and Jesus Christ. The same term is used as a self-designation by Paul (Rom 1:1; Phil 1:1; cf. Titus 1:1) and by the author of Revelation (1:1); and it is also used as a more general term for Christians (Acts 4:29; 16:17; Rev 1:1). It is significant that the author does not claim to be one of the twelve or, in contrast to Paul, to be an apostle (Rom 1:1; 1 Cor 1:1; 2 Cor 1:1; Gal 1:1; so also in Colossians, Ephesians, and the Pastoral Letters, works often considered to have been written in Paul's name). In other words, James does not claim any ecclesiastical authority other than that of a teacher (3:1-2). The fact that he does not try to establish his credentials suggests that his original audience would have known which James was meant, although this argument from silence is used both to prove and to disprove his authorship of the letter. For reasons given in the introduction, the implied author is James, the brother of the Lord and leader of the church in Jerusalem for nearly twenty years. Even if we do not believe that he actually wrote the letter, it is convenient to continue using "James" as a shorthand for the author. Nothing else in the letter speaks directly about the author's identity or his location at the time of writing.

He addresses his audience as "the twelve tribes in the Dispersion." The biblical description of the settlement in Canaan identifies the twelve tribes as the sons of Jacob. After the fall of the Northern Kingdom of Israel in 721 BCE and the Southern Kingdom of Judah in 587 BCE, leading citizens of the tribes were carried into exile and eventually came to be known as those living in the Dispersion or Diaspora. Later the term was extended to all Jews who chose to live outside the Holy Land. By the first century CE, large Jewish communities existed in such cities as Alexandria, Syrian Antioch and Damascus, and Rome, where they were much more exposed to hellenizing influences. Acts describes Paul's contact with such communities in the cities that he visited.

Does the phrase "the twelve tribes" tell us anything about the identity of James's audience? There are three major possibilities, each with some nuances. "Tribes" may refer to (1) ethnic Jewish communities; (2) Jewish-Christian communities, whom James understands to be the true successors of the tribes of Israel; or (3) the entire church, also understood as the new Israel. Assuming that this is a Christian document, the first solution is unlikely, since James makes no appeal for conversion. The last solution presupposes a late date for James when the distinction between Jewish and Gentile churches had been resolved or when Jewish Christianity was no longer a viable option. Such an inclusive view of the church is clear, for example, in 1 Peter and Ephesians. For James, however, the most likely solution is the second one. The letter was originally intended for those Jews who accepted the lordship of Jesus Christ, wherever they lived.

Does the term *diaspora* tell us anything about the location of James's audience? The same term appears in 1 Pet 1:1, where it is specifically addressed to Christians in the provinces of Asia Minor (Elliott 1981, 30-31). Thus 1 Peter broadens the term theologically (to represent the church as an inclusive community), but narrows it geographically (to the provinces of Asia Minor). James, however, mentions no specific location. It is tempting to see "dispersion" as a reference to those who were "scattered" by the persecution in Jerusalem (Acts 12:19). However, in the introduction I argued that the implied audience consisted of hellenistic-Jewish congregations wherever they might be located.

◊ ◊ ◊ ◊

As noted earlier, this opening verse is an important clue to John's theology. James affirms the lordship of God and Jesus Christ (cf. 1 Cor 8:6). The article is missing in both cases, so that some commentators read it as "Jesus Christ, God and Lord"; but such a statement about the divinity of Christ seems to reflect later christological concerns rather than the early confession that "Jesus Christ is Lord" (Phil 2:11) and its various permutations in the New Testament. The suggestion of some commentators that this verse and 2:1 were added to a previously Jewish document in order to "Christianize" it has no textual evidence to support it.

CHRISTIAN CHARACTER: GROWTH AND SINGLE-MINDEDNESS (1:2-8)

James begins at once to offer moral advice or exhortation, the technical word for which is *parenesis*. However disjointed or unconnected the units in this chapter appear to be at first glance, they introduce the themes that are then developed later in the letter. In one way or another, they all deal with the moral life that Christians are to develop and emulate.

The opening section (1:2-8) consists of two units that are closely linked in at least two different ways. One link is *thematic*. The first unit (1:2-4) shows how a person develops character by dealing with obstacles. The next (1:5-8) then demonstrates that true character requires single-minded devotion to God. Thus both units deal with Christian character. Another way of linking the two units is *stylistic.* There is a series of word-linkages, technically called sorites, which are obvious in the Greek text but not in English translations. A word in one verse (or even in part of a verse) is then repeated either by the same word or by a cognate form, thus creating a chain effect. "Greetings" *(chairein)* in 1:1 is related to "joy" *(charan)* in 1:2. "Faith" in 1:3 reappears in 1:6. A more immediate link is the word translated "endurance" in 1:3 and 1:4. The Greek word *teleios* occurs twice in 1:4, although in the NRSV it is translated once as "full" and then as "mature." Different forms of the word "lacking" link 1:4 and 1:5, while "asking" links 1:5 and 1:6. "Doubting" appears twice in 1:6. The words translated "like" in 1:6 and "expect" in 1:7 are not the same, but they sound very similar. Different words for "man" occur in 1:7 and 1:8, one a generic term and the other designating the male gender. All of these linkages can easily be understood in the context of oral communication, which is typical of wisdom and proverbial literature. Since presumably most of James's audience could not read, these mnemonic devices would help listeners to remember what they heard. The whole section is tightly constructed.

◊　◊　◊　◊

Testing Produces Character (1:2-4)

As we have seen, James typically addresses his audience as "my brothers" (1:2). In part, this phrase has a rhetorical function of establishing a close bond between him and his hearers/readers. The authority of the letter derives from the author's role as a teacher who is able to impart traditional wisdom as well as new insights into the meaning of what it means to be Christians.

He begins his discussion of Christian character by telling his audience to consider it "all joy" (the NRSV's "nothing but joy" conveys the same meaning) when they encounter various "trials" *(peirasmoi).* Apparently these trials will be externally imposed, but nothing is explicitly said about suffering or persecution. By way of contrast, 1 Pet 1:6-7 also speaks of rejoicing (not the same Greek word) and of maintaining *faith* in a time of *trials*. In that letter the audience is told to expect acute suffering (being tested by fire) but is promised an eschatological blessing "when Jesus Christ is revealed." Both emphases (suffering, apocalyptic) are absent, or at least muted, in James.

James clearly does not suggest that these trials are valuable for their own sake. Rather, they become the occasion by which Christians can grow in faith. The progression here begins with a testing of faith; the noun *dokimion* in 1:3, which usually has the sense of a means of testing, is to be preferred to manuscripts that have the adjective *dokimon*. This leads to "endurance" or "perseverance" *(hypomonē),* a characteristic of Christian virtue in Revelation (see 2:2, 3, 19; 3:10; 13:10; 14:12). For James, though, this endurance is not complete until it leads to perfection. The term *teleios* is repeated twice in 1:4. The first time it modifies the term *work*. In 2:22 it appears again in a verb form, combined with the same two words: "and faith was brought to completion by the works." The second time it is used in 1:4 it is complemented by another word with the same meaning *(holoklēros)* and the two terms are translated as "mature and complete." "Mature" does a better job of conveying to us James's concept of the development of character than the traditional word "perfect." The adjective "perfect" will also appear in 1:17 (God's "perfect gift") and in 1:25 ("the perfect law"). In this unit, then, the progression is: trials or tests of faith that produce endurance, which lead to maturity.

In some respects, the progression in Rom 5:3-4 is similar: suffering produces endurance, which produces character, which produces hope in God's grace. However, it is a mistake to read this passage of James in light of Rom 5, 1 Pet 1:6-7, and Matt 5:11-12 ("Blessed are you when people revile you and persecute you," etc.) as Davids (1982, 65-70) seems to do. All three of those passages focus explicitly on either suffering or persecution, or both, which are not mentioned in James. Also, all three of those passages occur within an apocalyptic setting: "for your reward is great in heaven" (Matt 5:12); "we boast in our hope of sharing the glory of God" (Rom 5:2*b*); and an inheritance kept in heaven awaiting the revelation of Jesus Christ (1 Pet 1:4, 7). In Jas 1:4 the idea of perfection may have an eschatological overtone, but it is not stated. The primary meaning seems to be much closer to the moral sense found in Matt 5:48: "Be perfect, therefore, as your heavenly Father is perfect." To put it differently, this unit in James does contain a teleology, a movement of growth in wisdom and in faith; but there is no explicit picture of divine judgment or reward.

The growth or progression described in these verses is not intended only for individual Christians. The community as a whole needs to develop the same discipline (Johnson 1995b, 183-84). For that reason, this unit anticipates the concluding verses of the letter (5:19-20), which stress the importance of bringing back another Christian from error and death.

In James the "trials" relate to two aspects of their situation that are spelled out in the next two units. One is their religious search for wisdom (1:5 and again in 3:13-18). Jewish wisdom literature frequently admits that there are many obstacles to its attainment. *Sirach* 4:17, for example, describes how Wisdom will treat a seeker; she "will torment him by her discipline" (RSV); cf. *T. Jos.* 2:4-7, which includes the comforting statement that God does not abandon those who are seekers or God-fearers. The other aspect is sociological. The crises and frustrations that James mentions, as we shall see, are a result of the fact that those who experience them are poor and marginalized (1:9-11; 2:5-7; 4:13–5:6).

God's Gift Demands Single-Mindedness (1:5-8)

In Greek the next unit begins emphatically with "but if" and addresses those who lack wisdom. The author's assumption is that many of those who hear his message will identify themselves as ones who need greater wisdom, a theme that anticipates 3:13-18. This unit is linked to the previous one by a repetition of the word "lack" (1:4). It immediately sets up a contrast between those whose goal is to lack nothing (1:4) and those hearers ("If any of you") who lack something essential, namely wisdom. The Wisdom of Solomon contains a remarkable parallel: "For even if one is perfect among the sons of men, yet without the wisdom that comes from thee he will be regarded as nothing" (9:6 RSV).

Verse 5 focuses first on God as giver; the verb *didōmi* occurs twice. This theme reappears in various forms in 1:17 (God as the source of every perfect gift), in 1:21 (the "implanted word"), and in 3:17 (God as the source of "wisdom from above"). The focus then shifts to the need to ask in faith, without doubting (1:5-6). James contrasts the person who never doubts and the one who does, using the same word twice in an identical form in 1:6; in the NRSV "the doubter" is repeated in 1:7 to make a smoother translation, even though the word does not appear in the Greek text. The adjective "double-minded" *(dipsychos)* appears in 1:8 for the first time in any literature; see also 4:8. The phrase "wretched are the double-minded" appears in *1 Clem.* 23.3-4 as part of a quotation from "scripture" and in *2 Clem.* 11.2-3 is cited from "the prophetic word." It also appears in different forms in *1 Clem.* 11.2 and *2 Clem.* 11.5, as well as more than forty times in the writings attributed to Hermas (particularly in *Herm. Man.* 9–10).

In contrast to 1:1, "the Lord" in 1:8 clearly refers to God the giver, not to Christ.

◊ ◊ ◊ ◊

The unit has a double focus. The first is on God as giver (1:5). We are told *what* God gives, namely wisdom. This view appears frequently in wisdom literature (e.g., *Wis* 7:7; 8:21; *Sir* 1:1; 17:11). We are also told *how* God gives: completely and without reservation (NRSV: "generously and ungrudgingly"). Finally, we learn *to whom* God gives. Our first impression is "to all" *(pasin),* which would make wisdom a universal gift from God and part of human nature, but the following verses make it clear that there are some conditions for receiving God's gift. (On wisdom in James see Felder 1982.)

In the rest of the unit (vv. 6-8), the focus shifts from God to the asker, and in particular to the way in which we should ask. The first condition is that we should ask in faith. This saying is strikingly similar to Jesus' teaching about prayer, notably in Matt 21:22

("Whatever you ask for in prayer with faith, you will receive") and Mark 11:24 ("So I tell you, whatever you ask for in prayer, believe that you have received it, and it will be yours"). Other parallels may be found in the saying ask/seek/knock (Matt 7:7 = Luke 11:17) and also in John 16:23.

Linked with the need to have faith when we ask God in prayer is another condition. We should not doubt! James reinforces that claim with two vivid images. If we doubt, we are like a wave during a storm at sea, tossed back and forth. In Wis 14:1-7 and in classical sources there are numerous references to a ship on a storm-tossed sea, but in this passage the focus is on the waves themselves. The image is a standard one in the wisdom tradition, but it would have particular meaning for anyone who had experienced such a storm. James uses it to show that such a person who doubts has lost control over his or her life and cannot expect any gifts from God. This image, then, contrasts sharply with the more serene picture of a ship and its rudder in 3:4-5. The other image is that of the person who is "double-minded and unstable in every way" (v. 8). The use of the term *dipsychos* has already been discussed, but there is one other striking parallel: "But those who are perfect in faith make all their requests trusting in the Lord, and they receive them, because they ask unhesitatingly, without any double-mindedness" (*Herm. Man.* 9.6). Dibelius describes this statement as "the best commentary on our v. 6" but stops short of seeing any literary dependence (Dibelius and Greeven 1976, 79-82).

In this opening section, then, James has given both positive and negative clues to developing Christian character. Faith (vv. 3 and 6) is the key to both units. When we are faced with trials, faith enables us to build up our endurance and so to mature (cf. 5:7-11). This is a process of growth in learning how to deal with unexpected challenges or personal hardships. Faith is also the key to developing a relationship to God in prayer, particularly when we ask for wisdom. To ask in faith means to practice an unswerving devotion to God. The negative example is that of the doubter, the person who is uncertain or insecure about his or her relationship to God.

TRUE REWARDS:
THE POOR AND THE RICH (1:9-11)

This section stands between the two parallel sections of 1:2-8 and 1:12-18. It is not tied closely to either of the others, but it does introduce the contrast between rich and poor, which is discussed in greater detail in 2:1-7, 14-16 and 4:13–5:6. Internally, the unit is linked by different forms of the word "lowly" (1:9, 10) and the words "flower" and "field" (1:10, 11). The image of withering and fading is clearly based on Isa 40:6f, which is quoted at greater length in 1 Pet 1:14.

In 1:9, the subject is a "brother," James's favorite word for a believer. This person is characterized as "lowly" *(tapeinos)*, which can refer either to one's social status or to one's attitude of humility, as in 4:6. Here being lowly implies poverty, since the counterpart in 1:10 is "a rich person" *(plousios)*, even though *tapeinos* is not the usual word for a poor person (cf. *ptōkos* in 2:2-6). In 5:15 the statement "the prayer of faith will save the sick, and the Lord will raise them up" picks up a theme from the previous section (1:5-6), and the theme of exaltation in this section (1:9), even though the same words are not used in each case.

◊ ◊ ◊ ◊

James encourages his audience to boast about the prospect of their elevation. Paul rejected boasting about human achievements as a kind of works righteousness, although he was willing to boast about his sufferings as the marks of a true apostle (e.g., 2 Cor 11:16-30; Gal 6:13-14) or in God's grace (Rom 5:2; 1 Cor 1:29-31). James is much more restrained, but apparently the text refers to a future reversal of fortunes similar to that found in the Magnificat (Luke 1:51-53) and in the Q saying about humility and exaltation (Matt 23:12 = Luke 14:11).

Who is this rich person? On the one hand, many commentators assume that it refers to a Christian, and so they supply the term "brother" in verse 10 even though it is missing from the Greek text. In other words, the "brother" (NRSV: "believer") of verse 9 is taken to apply to both the lowly (v. 9) and to the rich persons (v. 10). On the other hand, elsewhere in James the rich appear to be outsiders who exploit and oppress believers. This view is made explicit in 2:6-7, and it is more likely the view here.

In this passage much more is said about the fate of the rich than of the poor. There is no separation of the sheep and the goats such as we find in Matthew's Gospel, no apocalyptic vision or *parousia* scene like those in 1 Thess 4:13-18 or Rev 19:11-21. In James no such apocalyptic picture appears until chapter 5. Although an ultimate reversal of fortunes is clear, the disappearance of the rich is presented in terms of natural images: flowers that die from the scorching heat of the sun, or perhaps from the searing winds that blow off the desert for days at a time (cf. "the wind from the east" in Jer 18:17; see also Hos 13:15 and Jonah 4:8). The translation is made difficult because James is using words that appear rarely or not at all elsewhere in the New Testament (see, e.g., Laws 1980, 64-65). The sense, however, is clear. The rich will simply disappear, right in the middle of their daily activities. The term *poreia* can be understood literally as their travels, but the NRSV translation in the more general sense of "a busy life" is preferable. Notice that it is the rich person who passes away, not wealth itself.

The theme of this short section is the contrasting fates of the rich and the poor, the reversal of fortunes. It therefore has almost nothing in common with the saying "[God] makes his sun rise on the evil and on the good" (Matt 5:45), with which it is sometimes compared. Here the rising of the sun is attributed to natural causes, not directly to God; and the emphasis here is not on equality, but on the fate of the rich. The section is intended as encouragement for those who are poor, who apparently compose at least a majority of the audience for which James is writing.

CHARACTER:
GROWTH TOWARD DEATH
AND LIFE (1:12-18)

This section also consists of two units, which parallel those in the opening section of 1:2-8. The first (1:12-16) deals with the causes and effects of temptation. It is linked directly to 1:2-4 by three terms: trial or temptation *(peirasmos)*, endurance (here the verb *hypomeno*), and proving testworthy *(dokimon,* which was a variant reading in 1:3). This time the catchword "trial" shifts the focus from external sources to internal struggles. As a result, the progression or development reverses direction. Instead of movement toward maturity *(teleioi* in 1:4), desire leads inevitably toward death *(apokuei thanaton* in 1:15). The mood is tragic rather than comic.

Internally, the first unit is linked by variants of the *peirazo* stem, translated as "temptation" or "tempted" in the NRSV (1:12, 13 [four times], 14); by "desire" (1:14, 15); and by "sin" (in 1:15 [twice]). There is a striking contrast between those who receive the crown of life (v. 12) and the death of those who cannot resist temptation (v. 15).

The second unit (1:17-18) focuses on God as the giver of all gifts, especially that of a new birth. Thus it develops one of the themes of 1:6-8.

Two verses in this section are difficult to fit into a logical scheme. In verse 12, the word *peirasmos* seems to mean external "trials," as it did earlier, while beginning in 1:13 it shifts to internal struggles or "temptation." Thus some commentators link 1:12 to 1:8-11 as its conclusion; others treat it as an independent, isolated verse; and still others see it as the first verse of a new section. Since the shift in meaning appears to be deliberate, verse 12 is best seen as introducing the unit 1:12-16 as both a parallel and a contrast to 1:2-4. The other difficult verse is the stern warning in 1:16, which can be linked to either what precedes or what follows. It is better to see it as the conclusion of the unit 1:12-16 for two reasons. First, it reinforces the seriousness of the inability to control one's own desires, leading to death. Second, if taken with verse 17, it obscures the parallelism between 1:17-18 and 1:5-8, both of which empha-size God as gift-giver. In any case, it is transitional.

One interesting link between the two units is the unusual word for giving birth *(apokueō)* used in both 1:15 and 1:18, the first time with reference to desire and the second time with reference to God.

◊ ◊ ◊ ◊

The Causes and Effects of Temptation (1:12-16)

The unit begins with a beatitude or blessing (1:12; cf. 1:25), a familiar form in the later Hebrew literature (Ropes 1916, 150), in Jesus' teaching (especially in the Sermon on the Mount, Matt 5:1-12), and in Revelation (seven times). The final beatitude in Matt 5:11-12 includes a vivid description of persecution and an apoca-lyptic sense of urgency, but these are missing in James. Instead, in James the promise of a future reward, a crown of life, is more closely linked to the Jewish wisdom tradition (e.g., Wis 4:2). The crown image also appears in Rev 2:10 and 3:11, but again in those passages the apocalyptic fervor is much more intense than it is in James. In his time, a crown could have a variety of meanings, such as a royal headdress or a wreath for an athletic victor. Here it is clearly the reward for those who have demonstrated single-minded devotion to God, described in this verse as "those who love him." The subject of the verb "promised" is absent in the best Greek texts; some manuscripts emend it by adding either "the Lord" or "God." In any case, the verse assumes a covenant relationship between the God who promises life and those who obey the first commmand-ment to love God unreservedly.

Why are we tempted? To answer the question James uses a familiar rhetorical device. He introduces a hypothetical speaker (1:13) who accuses God. Occasionally we read about someone who has committed a serious crime with the explanation "God told me to do it." James simply rejects such an excuse. First, he denies that God is the source of our temptations (1:13; cf. *Sir* 15:11-12). The second half of that verse is difficult to translate, but the meaning is clear in the NRSV. God does not tempt people to do evil. Why not?

Because "God cannot be tempted by evil." If that is the case, how can we account for our capacity for evil? Why does the Lord's Prayer include a petition "Lead us not into temptation" (Betz 1995, 400)?

James therefore offers an alternative explanation. The source of temptation is our own desire *(epithymia)*. That term does not necessarily mean sexual desire or lust, though James develops a graphic picture of desire that seduces a person ("lured and enticed"), who then gets pregnant, and gives birth to sin. Sin then grows to maturity and gives birth to death (1:14-15).

In sharp contrast to 1:3-4, the sequence here is from desire to sin to death. The closest analogy is found in Rom 7:7-11, although there it is the law—specifically the commandment "You shall not covet"—which stimulates sin, which in turn leads to death. In James there is no reference to the law and no mention of sin having a power of its own. The connection between desire and death may help to explain the "withering away" of the rich man in the unit just preceding this one.

Earlier, James showed how character is perfected in persons who exhibit self-control and perseverance, whose lives are unified by their devotion to God. Now we see the opposite process at work. Those who blame God are like the doubters who are storm-tossed. They are conflicted by their own desires and lack self-control. Their fate is death. James ends with a warning to his beloved believers: "Do not be deceived" (v. 16).

God as the Giver of All Good Gifts (1:17-18)

These two verses contain a number of themes. The first is God as a giver, which runs throughout the unit. Verse 17 begins by using two separate words for giving. The NRSV treats them differently, distinguishing the act of giving from the gift itself, although both terms may have the same meaning. Each one is qualified, one as being good *(agathē;* NRSV: "generous") and the other as perfect. The fact that these gifts are both "from above" and "coming down" reinforces the claim that God is the source. God is the giver of wisdom (1:5); see also 3:17, where wisdom is "from above."

Presumably God is also the source of "the implanted word" (1:21), either directly or indirectly (through those who teach).

A second theme is the nature of God. God is described as "the Father of lights," a phrase that recalls the creation account (Gen 1:3-5; cf. Ps 136:7). In addition, God is said to be unaffected by change. The end of verse 17 is notoriously difficult to translate, especially since three of the words appear only here in the New Testament; from ancient to modern times efforts have been made to improve the text (Martin 1988, 29-30, note b; also 38-39). The references in this verse to "lights" and to a shadow suggest the cycle of day and night, especially since the rising of the sun was mentioned in 1:11. On the other hand, if "lights" is taken to refer to the creation of the stars (Gen 1:14-19) and their movement, the idea is that God does not change, in contrast to the continuous orbiting of solar and planetary bodies. That contrast between permanence and impermanence had a long history in Greek thought, and by the time of James it had influenced Jewish thinkers as well. On the other hand, nothing here suggests that his readers thought their lives were being determined by celestial powers; the epistle stands in sharp contrast to some of the issues addressed in Galatians and Colossians.

A third theme is that of God giving birth (1:18). This is not only a bold image for God; it is also a stunning contrast to 1:15, where the same verb is used for that desire that "gives birth to death." Here the image is modified in two ways. For one thing, the birth that God gave is not accidental or unwanted. It occurred deliberately or willingly, an adverb translated in the NRSV by the phrase "in fulfillment of his own purpose." Moreover, the birth was not the result of normal sexual intercourse but "by the word of truth." Once again we are reminded of the creation story in Genesis, which reports how God created by speaking. Elsewhere in the New Testament, the same image is most familiar in the prologue to the Fourth Gospel (John 1:1-18). The real question is whether James is speaking of the creation of all humanity, or whether "the word of truth" is the gospel that gives new life to those who respond in faith. For Paul, Christ's death and resurrection implied the death of the old humanity and the creation of a new one (e.g., Rom 5:12-21) or of a new creation (2 Cor 5:14-17, set within a larger context of the ministry of reconciliation); but James never mentions the death and resurrection of Christ. In John, *anōthen* refers to being "born again" or "born from above" (John 3:3, 7). In James, however, "from above" refers to God's gifts (1:17), while the birth is "by the word of truth" (1:18). Also, in John the new birth is by the Spirit (3:6, 8) or by water and the Spirit (3:5), but there is no mention of the Spirit in James. He simply does not develop the many possible dimensions of the birth image, but it does stand over against the earlier images of death in 1:11 and 1:16.

Finally, James speaks about the "first fruits" of God's creatures (v. 18). This term contains the same ambiguity as "birth by the word of truth." Does it apply to all humanity, or only to those who accept Jesus as Lord and Christ? In the Hebrew Bible, "firstfruits" refers to the beginning of the harvest, products that were to be set aside as sacrificial offerings to God. Nothing in James suggests a sacrificial context such as that. For Paul, Christ's resurrection constitutes the "first fruits" *(aparchē)* of a new humanity (1 Cor 15:20, 23); but there is no mention of the resurrection in James. Paul also uses this term to refer to those who have the gift of the Spirit (Rom 8:23) and to his first converts in a given location (Rom 16:5; 1 Cor 16:15). In Revelation, it refers to the 144,000 who have the names of Christ and God written on their foreheads (14:4). James's imagery is more subdued. At least in this verse we do not find the apocalyptic fervor of Paul or of John of Patmos. James presents Christian believers as constituting a new humanity, but without any explicit mention of the resurrection or life after death.

◊ ◊ ◊ ◊

These two verses, then, present a succinct "theology" or description of God: generous, creative, unsusceptible to constant change, purposeful, the fertile source of the word of truth, and creator of a new kind of humanity among those who have faith in him. The ethical implications of that "word of truth" will become clear in the section that follows.

DEVELOPING CHARACTER
THROUGH SELF-DISCIPLINE (1:19-27)

In verse 19 "my beloved brothers" once again marks the beginning of a new section, in which James argues that character develops through self-discipline. Within the section are three units. The first (vv. 19-21) focuses on communication, in both speech and act; the second (vv. 22-25) stresses the importance of acting and not just listening; and the third (vv. 26-27) defines the kind of action that true religion requires.

The link with the previous section is apparent. The declarative statement in verse 18 that we have been given birth by the *word of truth* is followed by hortative pieces of advice: *"welcome with meekness the implanted word"* (1:21 emphasis added) and *"be doers of the word,* and not merely hearers who deceive themselves" (1:22 emphasis added). Throughout this section, then, James is developing the ethical implications of the new birth.

Internally, the three units are linked in several ways. The word for "man" in verse 19 is the generic *anthrōpos,* while in verses 20, 23 it is the gender specific *anēr,* although for James both terms carry the meaning of "human." The listening that is stated in verse 19 and implicit in verse 21 (welcoming the implanted word) shifts to a focus on the "hearer" in verses 22, 23, and 25. The advice to be slow to speak (v. 19) is reinforced by the warning to bridle your tongue (v. 26). What it means to be "doers" in verses 23 and 25 (in two different forms) is defined at the end of the section (v. 27). The need to keep yourself unstained by the world (v. 27) was anticipated by the advice to rid yourselves of sordidness and wickedness (v. 21).

◊ ◊ ◊ ◊

Character and Communication (1:19-21)

Although some manuscripts open this verse with the word *hoste* ("therefore"), the preferable reading is *iste,* a verb meaning "to know or understand." Although it can be taken as an indicative meaning "you know," it is better to read it as an imperative, "know this" (NRSV: "You must understand this"), which balances the next verb ("let everyone be").

Self-discipline involves three things: being quick to hear, slow to speak, and slow to anger. The first two phrases include paired infinitives. Hearing and speaking both involve oral communication, a theme that will reappear not only in verse 26 but especially in 3:1-12. Both themes appear extensively in Jewish and hellenistic wisdom literature (for a list of sources see, e.g., Davids 1982, 91-92; Johnson 1995b, 199-200). An unusually close parallel appears in *Sir* 5:11: "Be quick to hear, and be deliberate in answering" (RSV). The third item in the sequence, anger, differs from the others in two respects. Grammatically, it is a noun (*orgē* in both vv. 19 and 20) rather than a verb, although the phrase *eis orgēn* can be translated "to anger." Thematically, it deals with communication as an act and not merely as speech. In Prov 29:11 it is a fool who cannot control anger; the wise person restrains it (cf. Sir 1:22-24). Both Plutarch and Seneca wrote long essays on anger. In the first of a series of antitheses ("You have heard that it was said . . . but I say") in Matt 5:21-22, Jesus identifies a threefold sequence from the act of murder to anger to insulting speech (disrespect). For Jesus, the loss of verbal self-control deserves the most serious punishment. It sets in motion a progression that may lead to murder. James clearly links anger and speech in this passage, and in 4:1-4 he links murder to our desires that get out of control. Character, then, means learning how to control the way we communicate, in both word and act.

Anger is futile, James reminds his readers, because it cannot produce God's righteousness (v. 20). The verb for "produce" *(ergazomai)* has the same root as the noun "works" *(erga),* so this verse anticipates 2:14-26, where the noun "righteousness" and the verb "justified" appear four more times (cf. 3:18 and the adjective "righteous" in 5:6, 16). In the New Testament, the phrase "the righteousness of God" can refer to what God *is;* that can hardly be the meaning here. It can also refer to what God *expects,* to the just demands spelled out in the Torah and elsewhere. That is a possible interpretation of this verse, but the more likely meaning is a third alternative: what God *gives* = justification, a right relationship to God. Anger is a character flaw that interferes with our relationship to God.

Verse 21 opens with an emphatic "therefore" and goes on to close this unit with two commands, one negative and one positive. The negative "rid yourselves" is actually a participle, but it has the force of an imperative. In Col 3:8 the same verb is used to introduce a list of vices, which incidentally includes two of the words used in this unit: anger *(orgē)* and wickedness *(kakia)*. Since the same word can be used for taking off your clothes, it is sometimes associated, either literally or figuratively, with a baptismal rite in the early church (Braumann 1962, Meeks 1974). The Christian is to put away all of those vices associated with the old person, here summarized in a series of rarely used words ("sordidness and rank growth of wickedness").

In Col 3:12, the positive command is to "put on" (literally to "clothe yourselves" with) Christian virtues, which are then listed. In James, the command is to receive (NRSV: "welcome") the "implanted word." The word is almost certainly the same as the "word of truth" in verse 18 and therefore a reference to the good news. What about the term "implanted," though? Remember our discussion about the wisdom that God gives "to all" in verse 5, since it dealt with the same issue? "Implanted" could mean that the word is part of our natural endowment, that is, it is innate. That hardly seems consistent with the images of being given birth and of being firstfruits in verse 18. The more obvious meaning, then, is that the implanting refers to the act of hearing and receiving the Christian message. The receiving is not a one-time event but a repeated process, as the next unit makes clear.

How should we receive the word? With meekness *(praütēs)*, James tells us (v. 21). Meekness, like humility, is a key to his view of Christian character. It is an important echo of the first beatitude (Matt 5:3), and not surprisingly it appears in New Testament lists of virtues like that of Col 3:12 (cf. also Gal 5:23; 6:1; Eph 4:2, in all three cases translated as "gentleness" in the NRSV). In contrast to our meekness, the word itself is powerful. In fact, James says, it has the power to change your souls (i.e., you as a person).

◊ ◊ ◊ ◊

This unit, then, shows the connection between communication and character. It begins with a command to be quick to listen and slow to speak, proceeds to identify anger as the act that keeps us alienated from God, urges us to get rid of everything that keeps us from growing in our devotion to God, and finally returns to the need to listen to that word of God that can deliver us. To be a Christian means to let go of our own sinfulness and receive God's word.

Character and Action (1:22-25)

From the last unit we might conclude that Christians don't need to do anything except listen to their teachers and preachers. In this new unit James destroys that illusion. Being good listeners or hearers is not enough; we must be doers as well (v. 22). The new unit clearly anticipates 2:14-26.

Centuries earlier, in his *Nichomachean Ethics,* Aristotle argued that character develops over time, as we develop the habit of deciding and acting morally. In his view, we become moral persons as we learn to avoid extremes and to act according to a mean. The idea of acting temperately became a staple of the hellenistic moral tradition. It is certainly part of the "thought world" of James (see the introduction). In addition, hellenistic influence on the Jewish tradition sometimes led to a blending of wisdom and the Torah (e.g., Sir 1:26: "If you desire wisdom, keep the commandments, and the Lord will supply it for you" [RSV]; cf. 19:20 and *T. Levi* 13:1-9). In other words, the law defined what it meant to act wisely. The latter seems to be the context for James's saying about the "word" (v. 22), which is almost certainly the equivalent of the "perfect law" (v. 25).

The theme is stated in the command to "be doers of the word, and not merely hearers who deceive themselves" (v. 22). Ezekiel scorns those who come to hear his words but don't put them into practice (Ezek 33:30-33). The rabbinic tradition in the Mishnah (*Aboth* 5:14) classifies people as those who hear the law and do not do it, those who do the law without hearing it, the pious person who does both, and the ungodly person who does neither. That debate is no doubt older than Jesus and James. It is reflected in sayings in the Sermon on the Mount about doing and teaching the commandments (Matt 5:19) and about hearers and doers (Matt 7:24-27; cf. 7:21), as well as here. One variant reads "hearers of the law," rather than of the "word," which may show the influence on a later copyist of that phrase in Rom 2:13. The word "deceiving" reminds us of the power of our desires (v. 14).

James then uses a powerful metaphor to illustrate the point of this unit, which is to be doers of the word and those who act on the "perfect law." The same verb for "look" *(katanoeō)* connects vv. 23 and 24. A person glances in a mirror and sees "the face of his birth"; a footnote in the NRSV accurately translates the Greek text. It could also be translated as his "natural appearance" (Davids 1982, 98) or "the face nature gave him" (Ropes 1916, 176). Some commentators think this refers to "the image of God" (see Gen 1:26-27); but that is doubtful since James implies that the look is just a quick one, and ancient mirrors of polished metal might distort the image. In the familiar passage in 1 Cor 13:12 ("For now we see in a mirror, dimly"), Paul contrasts our present blurred knowledge of God with what we can expect in life after death. James makes a different point. If all we do is to hear the word, then we are like those people who just glance in the mirror, go away, and forget how they look. The mirror image is a familiar one in wisdom literature (e.g., Wis 7:26; Sir 12:11). Ordinarily, as it does here, it implies some kind of moral failure (Johnson 1995b, 213).

In verse 25 the end of the unit is introduced with an emphatic "but" (*de,* as in 1:22). The verse is a complex one. First, in contrast to those persons we just met who simply glanced in a mirror, a new verb introduces us to people who gaze or stare into the law. Second, another new verb—which begins with the same prefix *(para-)*—reinforces an image of permanence. These people not only gaze at the law but persevere. Third, the internal structure of this unit now becomes clear. It moves from "be doers . . . and not merely hearers" (1:22) to "if any are hearers . . . and not doers" (v. 23) to those who are "not hearers who forget but doers who act" (v. 25). The shift is from forgetful hearers to active doers (cf. Sir 11:27). Fourth, the law is not pictured as a set of "do's" and "don'ts" but as "the perfect law of freedom." It is hard to decide exactly what that means. However, in the context of the sayings about the "word" in verses 21-22, it can hardly mean obedience to the entire Torah. Rather, it hints at a new interpretation of Jewish law, which we find in 2:8-13, Matt 5:21-48, and elsewhere in the New Testament. Fifth, verse 25 contains another beatitude or blessing for those whose good works deserve it. A striking parallel is found in Luke 11:28: "Blessed . . . are those who hear the word of God and obey it." The notion of being rewarded on the basis of "works" is a sensitive issue; we will return to it when we examine 2:8-13.

According to James, character develops not only by facing trials, or by being single-minded in our devotion, but by hearing and doing the word/law. But exactly what is it that we are supposed to do? James answers that question in the next unit.

Character and True Religion (1:26-27)

This short unit, which contains James's definition of religion, is a key one in the entire epistle. It concludes not just verses 22-27, but the entire first chapter. It could stand alone, since its vocabulary and ideas are presented for the first time. Yet it is linked to the preceding units by several themes: the importance of controlling one's speech (v. 26; cf. v. 19); the need to keep oneself "pure and undefiled" and "unstained by the world" (v. 27; cf. v. 21); and the importance of being a doer (v. 27; cf. vv. 22-25). At the same time, it anticipates much of the discussion in Jas 2, so we must regard it as a transitional unit.

◊ ◊ ◊ ◊

Verse 26 begins with a hypothetical "if," which we have already seen in verses 5 and 23; an emphatic "but" *(de)* has been added in a few manuscripts. The term "religious" or "religion," which appears three times in these two verses, appears in only two other passages in the New Testament. In Acts 26:5 it refers to Paul's background in Judaism, and in Col 2:18 it refers to a speculative philosophy. Another rare word is that for bridling or reining one's tongue, used only here and in 3:2. It is a vivid image of the need for self-discipline. So is the image of deceiving one's heart, which reminds us of the double-minded person in verse 8. In some contexts the word translated "worthless" implies idolatry (e.g., Wis 13:1-2), but that meaning is not apparent here. The point of the verse is that our religion is worth nothing unless we have integrity. Thus James has told us what religion is *not*.

Verse 27, on the other hand, gives us a positive picture of what James means by religion. There are at least four things we should note in the verse. First, the focus of religion is not ourselves but God, described in a unique phrase, which literally reads "before the God and Father," which modern versions translate in a variety of ways. Religion is not a means of personal gratification but a way of relating to God.

A second issue is that religion involves *purity*. That is a central moral demand in the Hebrew Bible, particularly as part of the sacrificial cult (e.g., Lev 19–22). Priests had to avoid contact with anything that might contaminate them, such as a corpse or a woman during her menstrual cycle. Sacrificial offerings also had to be unblemished. The term could also apply to moral purity, that is, avoiding vices that make a person unacceptable to God. Anthropological studies by Mary Douglas and others have shown how central the notion of purity is in most cultures. For James, the focus is on the moral rather than the cultic aspect of religion (Countryman 1988, 131-33).

Third, according to James, religion includes a very practical social concern for orphans and widows. He is drawing on a theme that appears in every division of the Hebrew Bible: Torah (e.g., Deut 10:18; 24:17), the prophets (e.g., Mal 3:5), and the writings (e.g., Job 29:12-13; Ps 10:18; Sir 4:10). Caring for widows continued to be a concern in the early church (e.g., 1 Tim 5:3-16). In James, it is not clear whether the recipients of this concern are limited to members of the community or whether outsiders may be included. Here the mention of the "distress" (*thlipsis*, often translated as "tribulation" or "suffering") seems to refer to their poverty, not to signs that the end of times is at hand.

Finally, readers are warned to keep themselves unstained by the world. This was already implicit in the general advice to keep themselves pure and undefiled; now a contrast with the world is made explicit. The world thus has a negative meaning, as it does in some Qumran documents and in the Fourth Gospel. Some commentators view this verse in James as a warning against the zealotism or Jewish nationalism that led to the revolt against Rome in 66 CE (e.g., Reicke 1964, 23-24), but the text itself does not allow us to be that specific. Keeping oneself unstained does not necessarily mean withdrawing from the world into a monastic existence. The thrust of James's advice is moral rather than sociological. Christians must find a way to live in the world without adopting its value system, as we will see in 4:4. That is the mark of the Christian character, which James has been describing throughout this first chapter.

◊ ◊ ◊ ◊

This concluding section (vv. 19-27) demonstrates that character develops only through self-discipline. The first unit focuses on communication, particularly on controlling our listening and our speaking and our anger. It involves getting rid of evil habits and receiving God's word. The second unit emphasizes the need to act on what we have heard from God's word, the perfect law or law of liberty. Finally, the third unit defines true religion in terms of self-discipline (controlling our speech) and of service (care for the oppressed).

CHRISTIAN MORALITY AND THE LAW (2:1-13)

Chapter 2 of James is much more tightly woven than what we have seen so far. Strong arguments can be made to treat the entire chapter as a single block. However, two clues in verse 14 (the familiar use of "my brothers" and a shift to the theme of faith and works) indicate that we should treat verses 1-13 and verses 14-28 as separate sections.

The first section (vv. 1-13) includes three units. One gives a specific example of what a Christian should not do: favor a rich person over a poor one (vv. 1-4). Next James draws on the listeners' own experience to explain why they should not do that (vv. 5-7).

The third unit (vv. 8-13) gives a different argument based on the law, which is called "royal" in verse 8 and a "law of liberty" in verse 13. Throughout the section there are a number of links. In the NRSV, the same word is translated "favoritism" in verse 1 and "partiality" in verse 9. The adverb "please" in verse 3 is the same one translated "well" in verse 8 and in adjectival form as your "excellent" name in verse 7. Stylistically, questions beginning with "if" *(ei)* appear in verses 8, 9, 11*b* as well as in verse 1 *(ean)*. Also, the word "for" *(gar)* is used in verses 1, 10, 11, 13. The first two units are linked by the words "faith" (vv. 1 [NRSV: "believe"] and 5) and "poor" (vv. 2, 3, 5, 6). The word "rich" in verse 5 is used metaphorically (rich in faith), while in verse 6 it refers to rich men like the one in verse 2, although the term was not used there.

◊ ◊ ◊ ◊

An Example of Christian Immorality (2:1-4)

The new section begins with the usual phrase "my brothers." As noted earlier, the only references to the "Lord Jesus Christ" occur in 1:1 and 2:1. Unfortunately, the reference here is an awkward one. Literally, it reads "the faith of our Lord Jesus Christ of glory," but grammatically it can best be translated with the NRSV as "our glorious Lord Jesus Christ." Does faith mean "the faith (in God) that Jesus Christ had" or "our faith in Jesus Christ"? Ordinarily we would take the second option, as the NRSV does. In this case, however, the first option may be better. Before we can make a final decision, we will have to see what James means by "faith" in other passages.

After the opening address, James asks a question, one of many rhetorical devices that appear throughout chapter 2. In this case the question "Do you really believe . . . ?" is phrased so that the expected answer is "No." What makes their belief so problematic? It is expressed in a word *(prosōpolēmpsia)* that appears here for the first time in the New Testament, usually translated as "favoritism" or "partiality." Only here and as a verb in verse 9 does it apply to humans; the other occurrences (Rom 2:11; Eph 6:9; Col 3:25) all refer to God's impartiality. Yet, any time a new word is introduced into a language, its meaning is not clear until we have either an explanation or an illustration. In this case we have both. The *explanation* is found in Lev 19:15, a portion of which reads "you shall not be partial to the poor or defer to the great; with justice you shall judge your neighbor." The new Greek word translates and combines Hebrew words found in that verse. Later in Jas 2:8 we will see a direct quotation from Lev 19:18b; and other allusions to Lev 19:12-18 appear in James (Johnson 1982). Therefore in verse 1 the Old Testament background of this word points us toward the discussion of the law in verses 8-13.

The *illustration* is introduced in verses 2-4. Verse 2 requires us to make several decisions, and James does not give us much help. First, is he describing an actual or a hypothetical situation? The word "if" suggests that James is using an example of something that might happen, especially if he is writing to several congregations. On the other hand, verses 6-7 almost certainly describe something that had actually happened to his readers, hinting that James is being realistic throughout this section (Martin 1988, 61). Even if the situation described in verse 2 has not yet happened to them, it will happen sooner or later. Second, what does the term "synagogue" mean? In Judaism of that period it meant a "gathering" or "assembly." It referred less to a particular building or place of worship than to the people who were gathered (Horsley 1995, 222-37). James apparently uses it in that same sense. However, it must refer to a Jewish-Christian congregation, even though "church" *(ekklēsia)* is used everywhere else in the New Testament, and James himself uses it in 5:14. Third, what kind of meeting was this? Synagogues were not simply places for worship and teaching; the assemblies also performed judicial and business functions. It is at least possible that James is describing a judicial hearing of some kind and not a meeting for worship (Ward 1969). Finally, who are the visitors on this occasion? They certainly do not seem like regular members of the congregation. The impression is that they were inquirers hoping to learn more about the Christian faith, especially since the term for the wealthy man *(plousios)* is not used elsewhere for a Christian person (Davids 1982, 108). If those churches were composed primarily of poor people it would have been natural for them to want to attract some wealthy members. The answers to the last two questions are really linked. If it was a hearing, then the protagonists were likely to be members of the congregation. Matthew 18:15-20 describes the procedures for such a hearing; cf. *Did.* 4:3. On the other hand, if the two men were outsiders and inquirers, then the meeting was more likely a worship setting.

Verse 2 also describes vividly the contrast between the two visitors. One wears expensive jewelry and clothes; the other is shabbily dressed and perhaps needs a bath. The focus of this unit is on the different responses. Someone in the congregation (an usher? an officer?) directs the rich person to a seat. There is no reason to assume that the ring and the fine clothes indicated a Roman official or noble, particularly if the metaphor originated in a Palestinian setting. The poor person is told either to stand off to one side or to sit on the floor (literally, "below my footstool"), an act of intimidation. Several manuscripts read "sit here," probably to add a nice balance to the "stand there." A similar example of showing favoritism toward the rich is found in Sir 13:21-23.

In verse 4 James drives home the point of his illustration with another rhetorical question ("Have you not . . . ?"); this time the expected answer is "Yes." The verse is tightly constructed. The words translated "distinctions" and "thoughts" both have the same prefix *(dia-)*, while the word "made distinctions" shares the same root as "judges." Unfortunately the meaning of the verse is not so clear for two reasons. The first concerns the verb "to make distinctions," which could just as well be translated "to discriminate." It can be either reflexive, referring to our ability to distinguish one thing from another; or it can have an active sense of discriminating against someone, of putting them down. Second, the same ambiguity is found in the phrase *en heautois.* It can mean "within yourselves," a kind of reflecting on good and evil, as the rest of the verse implies; or it can refer to a division within the congregation, as the NRSV translation "among yourselves" implies. In favor of the first interpretation, which we might call reflexive or internalizing, is the fact that in 1:6 the same verb was used to describe the person who is internally divided, who is not an integrated self.

The second interpretation is more judgmental in character. From the point of view of the rich person, the congregation's action was "favoritism"; but from the perspective of the poor person it certainly looked like discrimination (which is another possible translation for that word in 2:1). As a result of that act, the congregation was divided. The verses that follow, in which James reminds them of their treatment at the hands of the rich, lend support to this interpretation. Of course, it may be that the ambiguity is deliberate. For James, Christian morality should exclude both kinds of discrimination.

An Argument from Their Own Experience (2:5-7)

A new unit, addressed to "my beloved brothers," begins with an arresting imperative: "listen." It consists of three more rhetorical questions, each introduced by *ouk*, indicating that these are things that members of the congregation ought to know. The argument in this unit appeals to different aspects of their own experience.

The first question in 2:5 ("Has not God chosen the poor?") reminds them of what God has done; it is a theological argument. Two verbs control the sentence: God has chosen and God has promised. In James, God's election and not the death of Christ is the theological basis for Christian morality. It is a monotheistic assertion, as we might expect from a Jewish-Christian writer; but it affirms the priority of God's grace just as clearly as do Paul and other early Christian writers. The unexpected twist is that God has chosen the poor! The phrase "in the world" can mean "from the world's point of view." As noted in the introduction, a tradition of the "pious poor" had developed in Judaism. It is reflected in the "poor in spirit" in Matt 5:3, which may give us some insight into the character of the communities to which James was writing. On the other hand, "in the world" may refer to actual poverty, as the parallel version of the beatitude in Luke 6:20 suggests. If so, these are clear statements of a "preferential option for the poor" so prevalent in contemporary liberation theology (e.g., Hanks 1992; Tamez 1990).

Why, then, has God chosen the poor? For two reasons. The first is so that they might be rich in faith. A similar sentiment is found in the Jewish tradition: "The man who is poor but free from envy, who is grateful to the Lord for everything, is richer than all, because he does not love the foolish things that are a temptation common to mankind" (*T. Gad.* 7:6). James does not value poverty for its own sake. Rather, it is an opportunity for personal and collective growth of the kind that we saw in 1:2-4. In contrast, Paul speaks about God's election of the poor and weak in 1 Cor 1:26-31 in a very different context (the cross) and with a different purpose (to transform the world's value system and to prevent people from boasting in their own achievements). The second reason is so that they might be *heirs* of God's *kingdom,* two key words appearing here for the only time in James. There is a striking similarity to Jesus' beatitude (Matt 5:3), but the absence of such language elsewhere in James shows that a futuristic or apocalyptic hope was not the main priority in his teaching. It is present, to be sure, but it is not the controlling framework of James's message. In contrast, Matt 31:34 promises God's kingdom in a context of a final judgment scene that condemns some to eternal punishment and others to eternal life. The final phrase in Jas 2:5 ("to those who love him"), which we saw earlier in 1:12, is now applied to the Christian poor.

The first clause in verse 6 really concludes the theme of verse 5, and indeed of the unit 2:1-4 as well. If they show favoritism or discrimination they dishonor the poor whom God has chosen. This is the lesson they should learn from this story of their immorality.

Three more rhetorical questions in verses 6-7 also appeal to the audience's experience, this time providing a sociological rather than a theological argument. James reminds his audience that at least some of them did, in fact, suffer as a result of three actions. Some rich people oppress them, drag them into court (v. 6), and discredit their good name (literally "blaspheme" in v. 7; see also 1 Pet 4:14; cf. "cast out your name as evil" in Luke 6:22, an alternative but accurate reading in the NRSV). However, on the basis of this limited evidence it is not possible to identify these rich persons as financiers (cf. Maynard-Reid 1987, 63-64). Their good (NRSV: "excellent") name almost certainly refers to their designation as followers of Christ (whatever name that may have been) and not to their individual reputations. No doubt this included the kind of verbal harassment that minority groups often have to endure; but it may also have affected the ability of Christians to engage in trade.

An Argument Based on the Law for Christians (2:8-13)

Once again there is a shift, both stylistic and thematic, while maintaining continuity with the last two units. The new unit is marked by a series of conditional sentences introduced by "if" (*ei* in vv. 8, 9, 11*b*), which do not imply hypothetical situations, but real options open to James's readers. Similarly, the term "for" *(gar)* appears three times (vv. 10, 11, 13). The conjunction *de* appears once in verse 9 and twice in verse 11; the first and last uses, translated "but," are adversative; they set two different situations in sharp contrast to each other. The theme of this unit is the role of the law in the Christian life. Specifically, this argument shows that the law *(nomos)* is the scriptural basis for our obligation to care for the poor. Thus it provides a third rationale to the theological and sociological arguments of the last unit.

◊ ◊ ◊ ◊

The initial "if" of verse 8 is followed by the word *mentoi*. It can mean simply "however," which would be consistent with other New Testament usage (Davids 1982, 114; so NEB). This context seems to demand the more emphatic translation "really" (so NRSV, NIV). Four things are worth noting in this verse. The first is the designation of the law as "royal," similar to the modifier "perfect" in 1:25. Why is it royal? The obvious answer is that it comes from God, the king of the universe. Possibly there is an implicit reference to Christ, the Lord, as an interpreter of the Torah. This is a view that permeates Matthew's Gospel, but it represents a later development. James does not explicitly claim such authority for Jesus.

Second, James refers to "scripture," but what does he mean by that? During the first century CE, Judaism accepted the Torah and the prophetic books as sacred texts. Beyond that no consensus existed about which books were eventually to be included within the third section of the Hebrew Bible known as "the Writings."

Books that are now part of the Apocrypha and Pseudepigrapha enjoyed popularity within different parts of the Jewish community, as the library at Qumran makes abundantly clear. Which books have the authority of Scripture for James? It obviously includes the Torah, since he quotes Leviticus in this verse and Genesis in verses 21-23 (cf. 3:9). None of his other citations from biblical books are identified as having the same authority. In addition, James contains a number of allusions to the Jewish wisdom tradition and frequent parallels to sayings of Jesus; but James never identifies them as Scripture. Apart from the Torah, the limits of James's canon remain vague.

Third, as an example of the law, James cites Lev 19:18b: "You shall love your neighbor as yourself." The wording is taken directly from the Septuagint (LXX), the Greek translation of the Hebrew Bible. According to Matt 22:37-39, when Jesus was asked to give a summary of the Torah—that is, when he was asked to choose the verse(s) that summed up all the rest of the commandments—he combined this verse with a portion of the familiar *Shema* in Deut 6:5: "You shall love the LORD your God with all your heart, and with all your soul, and with all your might" (cf. Mark 12:29-31). Interestingly enough, when other New Testament authors cite the love commandment, they cite only the second half of Jesus' summary (Rom 13:9; Gal 5:14; and the Johannine references to a "new commandment" in John 13:34; 15:12; 1 John 2:7 and 3:11). James does exactly the same thing. "Here, indeed, it is explicitly commended as authoritative because it is scriptural, not because it is a command from Jesus" (Furnish 1972, 177; see 177-82 for his discussion of James's ethic). Nevertheless, in all of these citations it is hard not to see some influence of Jesus' own choice of that verse as a summary of Torah. In this case the citation gives a biblical basis for Christian morality. It is one more reason why Christians should not discriminate against the poor.

Finally, the verse ends with a commendation of his audience, in contrast to the condemnation in 2:6a. If you keep the royal law, he tells them, you do well. Unfortunately, we are left with some nagging questions, which do not need to be read in light of Paul's struggles with the law. Is it really possible to keep the law? How much of it are Christians obligated to keep? James has anticipated those questions, since he proceeds to answer them in verses 9-12.

Abruptly James returns to a note of warning. "But if you show partiality" (v. 9) is the prodasis or condition, a deliberate contrast to "if you really fulfill the royal law" in verse 8. The word for partiality is the same one that introduced the entire section in 2:1. Now, however, it is clear that partiality or discrimination is a violation of the law in general and of the love commandment in particular. The apodosis or conclusion of the sentence is found in two statements: "you commit sin and are convicted by the law as transgressors." The declarative verb "commit" is normally translated as "work." As in 1:20, the only other occurrence of the verb in James, it carries a negative meaning. It also prepares us for the discussion of "works" in the next section of the letter. "Convicted" is actually a past participle, though in the NRSV it is paired with "commit." Those who discriminate, then, sin; they are transgressors (a term repeated in 2:11).

In a sense, verses 10-12 are a digression. They attempt to answer the question "How much of the Law should Christians obey?" and to show that neglecting the poor is just as serious as breaking any other commandment. Verse 10 shifts from the second person of verses 8-9 ("if you"), to the more abstract third person ("whoever") in order to state a general principle: Anyone who fails at any point is guilty of breaking the whole Law (cf. T. Asher 2:5-10). It is stated even more forcefully in Matt 5:18-19 in a christological context, which apparently reflects Matthew's view of Jesus as a unique interpreter of the Torah. In Gal 5:3, Paul agrees that anyone who submits to the law must obey all of it, but he draws the negative conclusion that perfect obedience is an impossible condition for obtaining God's righteousness. There are two crucial issues here. The first is to determine what James means by keeping "the whole law." In verse 11 he gives an illustration based on the assumption that God is the lawgiver ("the one who said"). Returning to the second person, the verse says that even if you have never committed adultery, but you have murdered someone, you are guilty of breaking the commandments. The order of the commandments (adultery followed by murder) corresponds to the Septuagint version of Deut

5:17-18 (so also in Luke 18:20 and Rom 13:9, in contrast to Matt 19:18 and Mark 10:19). A striking link between James and the Sermon on the Mount is that the same two commandments appear in the so-called antitheses or contrasts in Matt 5:21-30 (where there they follow the traditional order found in the Hebrew Bible) even though they are missing from Luke's Sermon on the Plain. All of these New Testament citations refer only to the last part of the Decalogue, often called the second table of the law. In other words, they relate to love for the neighbor. The phrase "if you murder" is hypothetical, but it is still surprising; James will return to it in 4:2. None of this really tells us what James means by "the whole law." He never appeals to cultic or ritual requirements, so he cannot be classified with the circumcision faction whom Paul condemns in Galatians. Rather, throughout this letter, the impression we get is that "the law" for James refers to its moral requirements. It remains a guide to Christian morality.

The other key issue is whether this letter treats keeping the law as a condition for salvation. The answer is not at all obvious. For one thing, in this unit full obedience to the law has a positive rather than a negative value. The law is not a burden but is rather "the law of liberty" (v. 12, as in 1:15). That is, the intent of the law is not to produce universal sinfulness (in contrast to Rom 3:9-20), but to liberate. Here again the emphasis is on both speaking and acting, so that verse 12 looks back to 1:22-25 and forward to 2:14-26. For another thing, verse 13 (reverting to third person) implies that God as judge will show mercy on those who have shown mercy to their fellow human beings. That theme already existed in Judaism (Ecclus 3:10; 40:17; *T. Zeb.* 5:3; 8:1-3, especially "You also, my children, have compassion toward every person with mercy, in order that the Lord may be compassionate and merciful to you" in v. 1). It is prominent in Jesus' teaching (Matt 5:7) and is developed as a major theme in that Gospel (e.g., 9:13; 12:7; 18:23-35; 25:34-46; Hays 1996, 99-104). In the context of this whole section, then, the implication is that acting on behalf of the poor is an act of compassion that will provoke God's mercy.

◊ ◊ ◊ ◊

This entire section deals with an issue that James considers fundamental to Christian morality: the treatment of the poor. The three units are linked primarily by the warning not to show partiality. The opening verse (2:1) states that partiality is incompatible with faith in Christ, suggesting that those who discriminate are hearers and not doers of the law (picking up themes found in 1:22-25 and also in 1:27). The central unit implies that those who make distinctions have dishonored the poor (v. 6). The third unit is even more blunt. Those who show partiality "commit sin and are convicted by the law as transgressors" (v. 9). At issue is the question of justice tempered by mercy. It is no accident that the first unit ends with the observation that those who make distinctions have "become judges with evil thoughts" (v. 4), while the final verse of the section includes the statement that "judgment will be without mercy to anyone who has shown no mercy" (v. 13). The theological foundation for the author's argument is the conviction that "God has chosen the poor in the world to be rich in faith" (v. 5).

CHRISTIAN MORALITY AS FAITH IN ACTION (2:14-26)

The reasons for treating this as a new section have already been given: the stylistic address "my brothers" to mark a new beginning; and the shift of focus from favoritism (the poor and rich) to faith and works, a theme anticipated in 1:25. The section contains two distinct units, although they are closely related. In the first unit, the phrase "What good is it?" appears at the beginning (v. 14) and again in verse 16, providing a rough frame for the unit. "If" *(ean)* is repeated in verses 14, 15, and 17. In the NRSV the negative *mē* is translated "not" in verses 14 and 16 and "no [works]" in verse 17; it also introduces the question "Can faith save you?" in verse 14, indicating that a negative answer is expected. The second unit (vv. 18-26) begins with an emphatic "but." Once again an anonymous "someone" *(tis)* appears, as in verses 14, 16, but the style changes to a dialogue, perhaps even a challenge to James. In his response, James uses two Old Testament characters, Abraham and Rahab, as examples of faith expressing itself in works. Both units conclude with a statement that faith without works is dead, expressed slightly differently in each case (vv. 17, 26; cf. v. 20). At the same time, the entire section is connected to the first half of the chapter. The question "Do you really believe?" in verse 1, and the issue of favoritism, both anticipate the discussion of faith and works. Also, the word *kalōs* in verse 19 was used in verses 3, 7, and 8; the almost identical phrase "You do well" appears in verses 8 and 19, even though in the second instance it is meant more ironically.

Throughout the entire section, James tries to show that the development of Christian character requires both believing and acting, just as in 1:22-25 it required both hearing and doing. The issue is not whether faith or works is more important, but rather that both are indispensable.

◊ ◊ ◊ ◊

Faith Requires Action (2:14-17)

In good rhetorical style, James opens this new section with questions (v. 14). What is the advantage of having faith unless you put it into practice? Can faith by itself save you? It is clear that Paul and James were dealing with different issues. Paul's position apparently developed in opposition to the requirement that Gentile-Christian converts must accept the demands of the Torah, particularly those commandments dealing with circumcision and food laws. By way of contrast, his argument is that obedience to the law does not give Christians any advantage; faith in Christ is enough to put a person right with God (e.g., Gal 2:15–5:15; Rom 2:17–3:8). For James, on the other hand, the real issue is whether making a Christian commitment is worth anything unless it changes the way in which you live. Paul shows concern about the conditions for admitting Gentiles into the church; James is more concerned about Christian morality, about putting faith into practice.

In order to dramatize his concern, James gives an example that may be purely hypothetical; but it may also have been just as real in his day as it is today (vv. 15-16). His focus is on Christians who express concern, but who do nothing to improve the condition of the poor and the oppressed. The victims are naked and starving; in other words, they are desperately in need of clothing, food, and shelter. Moreover, they are not strangers but "a brother or sister," members of the community. Under the guise of Christian charity, some individuals in the church offer a blessing ("Go in peace") and yet "do not supply their bodily needs" (v. 16). This seems to violate James's definition of true religion (1:27). The lack of daily food may be reminiscent of the Lord's Prayer (Matt 6:11; Luke 11:3) even though the wording is different (cf. also the concern about daily necessities in Matt 6:25). The absence of clothing ("naked" in v. 15) is probably an exaggeration, but in the context of discrimination against the poor person with shabby clothes (vv. 3-4), the example gains added poignancy. Such neglect flies in the face of the commandment to "love your neighbor as yourself" (v. 8) and the opportunity to show mercy (v. 13). At Qumran, the sharing of goods and personal property was a requirement for full membership in the community (1QS), and Luke suggests that a similar requirement applied to the original Jerusalem church (Acts 2:44; 4:32). The letter of James does not imply a similar requirement, but it does imply that failure to provide for those in need undermines the ethos of the entire community. It leads to the conclusion in verse 17: without works or deeds or actions, faith is dead. The pithy conclusion is similar to adages such as "The proof of the pudding is in the eating" and "Put your money where your mouth is."

Faith and Action Are Inseparable (2:18-26)

The second unit (vv. 18-26) begins with a statement of the thesis, presented in dialogue form (vv. 18-19), followed by two examples from Scripture (vv. 20-25), concluding with a repetition of the summary slogan (v. 26).

◊ ◊ ◊ ◊

The opening verse of the unit (v. 18) creates one of the thorniest problems in the New Testament, one that cannot be separated from the verses that follow. James is using a familiar diatribe style. Normally it introduces a foil or an antagonist, a person who makes a statement in direct opposition to the author so that the latter can refute it. In this case, the problem is that the terms of the debate seem to be reversed. The words of the anonymous speaker "You have faith and I have works" actually represent the position of James; it is not a challenge at all. Thus the response in the second half of verse 18 ("Show me your faith apart from your works") completely misses the point. We have to remember, however, that in the early Greek texts there were no punctuation marks. We don't know where the quotation ended, and we can't even be sure whether the quotation was a statement or a question. Because of the confusion, there have been a number of ingenious solutions, none of them winning the support of a majority of scholars. Key issues are how to interpret the force of the first word *alla* and how to explain the apparently hostile response in verse 18 ("you sense-less person," or as we would probably say "you idiot" or "you jerk"). One solution is to treat the quotation as coming from an anatagonist but to end it after "You have faith," so that "I have works" becomes part of the author's reply. A second solution, which also treats the quotation as hostile, extends it through the end of verse 18 or 19 or even 20. A third solution treats the initial *alla* not as adversarial but as having a more neutral sense. It suggests that the speaker is actually an ally; he states exactly the position that James wants to defend, that is, he puts words in James's mouth. A fourth view is that the statement is purely hypothetical and is not directed to James at all. All four positions, and their variants, have their own strengths; but they also have problems that are grammati-cal or contextual or both (e.g., see Martin 1988, 76-78 and 86-88). I support the last option, cautiously rather than enthusiastically; but the important point is for you to be aware of the issues and work them through to your own conclusions.

The problem raised by verse 18 is partly resolved when we realize that James's response deals with two different issues. First, assum-ing that the hypothetical speaker said "You have faith and I have works," we can see that the statement forces a separation between faith and works. It hints that Christianity can be reduced to one or the other. James quickly rejects that possibility; faith and works are inseparable (v. 18*b*). True faith cannot exist apart from actions. The best manuscripts read "apart from" *(chōris),* although some read "from" *(ek);* the meaning is not substantially different. Second, his response shows that works can demonstrate a person's faith, while the reverse is not true. In effect, James is saying "How do I know what you believe unless it is expressed in your daily living, in your whole lifestyle?" That is what character is all about. Today we often use the term "cognitive dissonance" to describe a person whose belief system and actions do not coincide. The need for expressing one's faith in action has already been implied in 1:27; 2:15-16, 18, and 2:15-16. This theme, that we are "justifed by deeds, not by words" is repeated in *1 Clement* (30.3; see Penner 1996, 67-69).

A third issue appears in verse 19, but it is directly related to the last point. True faith is not an intellectual exercise. Rather sarcastically, James commends his foil for accepting the famous *Shema* of Deut 6:4, the first great commandment according to Jesus' summary (Mark 12:29), which was presupposed, but not mentioned in verse 8. The preferred textual reading is "that God is one" rather than the alternative "that there is one God." The implication, though, is that the other person's faith is nothing more than assent to a proposition. Even demons can acknowledge the existence of God. This is the first mention of demonic powers in James. We can assume that his readers would have taken their existence for granted, but the letter does not have a developed demonology. The description of them shuddering suggests strongly an exorcism context like those in the Gospels, where the demons recognize Jesus and the possessed person is convulsed both before and during the cure (e.g., Mark 1:24-26; 5:1-13; Luke 4:34-35).

The next verse (v. 20) is a transition from the dialogue to demonstrations. "Do you want to be shown, you senseless person" is typical of the diatribe style, both in the offer of proof and in the insult to the other person's intelligence. We might say "Do you need proof?" or "What do you need in order to convince you?" The phrase "faith without works" links this verse with verses 18 and 26. In verses 17 and 26 the conclusion is that such faith is "dead"; here it is that such faith is useless. Actually this is a play on words in Greek, since the term for works *(erga)* in verse 20 is followed immediately by the word *argē,* translated "barren" in the NRSV.

The first example that James uses is that of Abraham. Many commentators assume that he is revising or opposing Paul's interpretation of Abraham in Gal 3–4 and Rom 4. Actually, James is much closer to the Jewish tradition; Paul's view is an aberration. There is no need to read James through the eyes of later theologians who made Paul normative, nor do we have to assume that one author was trying to correct the other one (Ward 1968).

Stylistically the person in verse 20 is reminded of the point of this example not once but twice: by "you see" *(blepeis)* in verse 22 and "you see" *(horate)* in verse 24. In other words, the flow of the argument is:

(a) 2:21: the action by which Abraham expressed his faith = his willingness to sacrifice his son Isaac (Gen 22:1-18);

(b) 2:22: the application of that lesson = "his faith was active along with his works";

(c) 2:23: a text that proves that Abraham had faith in God and was justified (Gen 15:6);

(d) 2:24: the general application = "a person is justified by works and not by faith alone." The sequence "by works" followed by "not by faith" reflects the flow of the argument in these four verses.

Several other points are worth noting. First, Abraham is called our ancestor (literally "our father") in verse 21. Abraham as the father of Israel, both spiritually and ethnically, was recognized in Scripture (Isa 51:2) and in later Jewish tradition (e.g., Sir 44:19, 22). It would be a natural expression in a Jewish-Christian milieu. The same can be said about the phrase "friend of God" in verse 23, although it does not correspond exactly to any known text (Ropes 1916, 222-23; Martin 1988, 94). It probably anticipates 4:4, where James describes friendship with the world as enmity with God; such friendship stands in sharp contrast to Abraham. Luke Timothy Johnson (1995b, 243-44) has an extensive list of references to friendship in the Greco-Roman philosophical tradition, where it is stronger than in the biblical and later Jewish tradition. The designation of Abraham as "friend" is echoed in *1 Clem. 10:1*.

Second, as already noted, works and faith are not alternative paths to being justified by God, as Paul suggested in his polemic against "works of the law." In the original Greek this point is captured in a wordplay in verse 22 in which James says that Abraham's faith was "working with" *(synērgei)* his "works" *(ergois)*. Abraham's act of obedience to God in Gen 22 was the completion or perfecting of his faith (v. 22). It is not hard to see Abraham as an illustration of the testing of faith that grows toward maturity and completion (1:3-4). The phrase "justified by works" in verse 21 does not accurately reflect the argument of this unit, and it should not be taken out of context.

Third, the quotation from Gen 15:6, taken almost verbatim from the LXX, was used in its original context to refer to Abraham's willingness to believe that God would give him an heir. By applying it to Gen 22, the binding of Isaac or 'Aqedah in the Jewish tradition, James demonstrates the linkage between faith and the willingness to act.

Fourth, the second summary in verse 24 is directed not just to the protagonist of verse 18. By shifting to second-person plural James includes his readers as well. The verse is often taken as a crux of the disagreement between Paul and James, but that is a mistake. For one thing, the phrase "faith alone" *(pisteōs monon)* does not appear in Paul's work. Similarly, the Pauline phrase "works of the law" does not appear in James. They are dealing with different issues.

The other example that James uses is Rahab, who gets only one verse (v. 25). Her story, of course, is told in Josh 2:1-21. She welcomed Israelite spies who were casing the city of Jericho and hid them. Then, after expressing her faith in the God of Israel, under the cover of darkness she let the spies climb down a rope on the outside of the city wall so that they escaped. Later, when the city was captured by the Israelites, she and her family were spared (Josh 6:22-23). Thus she served as an example of a Gentile who embraced Israel's God.

The mention of Abraham and Rahab in the same passage is found also in Hebrews, especially 11:17-18 (the sacrifice of Isaac) and 11:31 (Rahab), and in *1 Clem.* 10–12. The latter, which may be dependent on James (Johnson 1995b, 74), develops the theme a step further by using both characters as examples of the way in which faith is demonstrated through acts of hospitality (*1 Clem.*

10:7 and 12:1). In James there is no explicit mention of Abraham's hospitality. However, the hospitality of Rahab, a non-Jew whose faith in God remains implicit in the text, gains meaning in light of the definition of true religion (1:27), the love command (v. 8), and the failure of some Christians to love their neighbors (vv. 15-16).

◊ ◊ ◊ ◊

As we have seen, the conclusion of this section in verse 26 ("faith without works is also dead") has already been stated in different forms in verses 17 and 22. What this verse adds is an analogy, almost certainly based on Gen 2:7, in which God's breath creates a living being. "For just as the body without the spirit is dead" is not a reference to the Holy Spirit, which is never mentioned in James. Rather the spirit is seen as the vital force that makes the difference between life and death.

In this section, it becomes clear that Christian character demands a faith that is active in love. Just as those who hear the word but fail to act on it deceive themselves (1:22), those who have faith but not works are dead (vv. 14-17). Specifically, faith demands acting on behalf of those who are in need (vv. 15-16). Moreover, a distinction between faith and works is not a viable option for James; one entails the other (vv. 18-26). For James, then, a faith that does not express itself in practical actions is lifeless.

Controlling Speech as a Test of Character (3:1-12)

At first glance, the entire chapter (3:1-18) seems to be a self-contained section dealing with teaching (Ropes 1916, 226-51). On closer inspection, however, there are almost no verbal or stylistic links between verses 1-12 (which focus on speech) and verses 13-18 (which focus on wisdom). Most other commentators treat these units together only as subheadings within a larger theme. Furthermore, chapter 3 is not directed only to teachers; they are not the only ones who need to learn how to control their speech. The various examples of speech getting out of control are addressed to a wider audience, the "my brothers" of verse 12. (Similarly, the description of true wisdom in vv. 13-18 is addressed to "anyone" in the congregation [v. 13] who thinks he or she is wise and has understanding, not just to a special class of sophists.)

For a variety of reasons, including some to be explained later, it is preferable to treat verses 1-12 as a complete section. It is unified in a number of ways. Verbally, the vocabulary contains a large number of words that appear rarely or not at all in other New Testament writings. What follows is a list of those words as they appear in the NRSV translation.

Words appearing only in this passage: guided (v. 4); boasts (v. 5); forest (v. 5); set ablaze (v. 5); set on fire (v. 6, twice); cycle (v. 6); reptile (v. 7); sea creature (v. 7); deathly (v. 8); pour forth (v. 11); opening (v. 11); salt (v. 12).

Words appearing only in James: bridle (v. 2; cf. 1:26); restless (v. 8; cf. 1:8 = unstable); poison (v. 8; cf. 5:3 = rust); brackish (v. 11; cf. 3:14 = bitter).

Words appearing fewer than five times in the New Testament: make mistakes (v. 2, twice); guide (vv. 3, 4); so large/very small (v. 4, the same word with opposite meanings); strong (v. 4); drive (v. 4); rudder (v. 4); will (v. 4); stains (v. 6); tamed (v. 7); curse (v. 9); cursing (v. 10); sweet (v. 11; NRSV: "fresh").

The meaning of many of these words, then, can only be determined by their use in noncanonical texts, most of which (such as bridling a horse, steering a ship, or a dealing with a fire that quickly spreads out of control) appear as examples in gnomic or wisdom literature (e.g, Dibelius and Greeven 1976, 185-90). Stylistically, the section is framed by verses 1 and 12. Both are addressed to "my brothers," which is used also in verse 10. Both begin with the interrogative particle *mē,* even though it is used differently in each case (and note the related *mēti* in v. 11). Throughout the section there is an artistic repetition of words and phrases, but we will note these as we go along. Virtually none of this language reappears in verses 13-18.

The section does not introduce a brand new theme, however. We were prepared for it by the advice about being slow to speak (1:19), about bridling the tongue (1:26), and about speaking and acting as those who are to be judged by the law of liberty (2:12). Moreover, the phrase "the whole body" *(holon to sōma)* appears at the end of verses 2 and 3, although in the NRSV it is translated "bodies" the second time to make it agree with the plural "horses," and is again mentioned in verse 6. It is striking that these verses follow so closely the statement that "the body *(sōma)* without the spirit is dead" in 2:26; there is a word association even if the ideas are not the same.

The main point in verses 1-12 is the need for self-control, but logically the argument is hard to follow. It opens with a warning against becoming teachers (v. 1), followed by the negative conclusion that we all fail (v. 2*a*). However, the second half of verse 2 shifts to a positive note: perfection involves the ability to control both speech and body. Two metaphors show that such control is possible, even in difficult situations such as taming a wild horse (v. 3) and steering a ship in a strong wind (v. 4). A third image portrays the tongue as a small fire (v. 5*a*), as though it is going to illustrate the same point; but immediately it shifts to a negative conclusion with another metaphor of the tongue as a world of iniquity by which evil can corrupt us (vv. 5*b*-6). Then a fourth image returns to the positive theme that virtually all animal life can be tamed (v. 7), only to draw the negative conclusion that the tongue is beyond human control (v. 8). The next point drives home the duplicity of human speaking (vv. 9-10), yet the illustrations that follow show that the natural environment has no place for such behavior (vv. 12-13). Given these apparently contradictory arguments, about the only sure conclusion we can draw is that our lack of self-control is against nature. This particular section, then, shows the influence of hellenistic thought more than any other in the letter; but by itself it does not help us to determine the author, the setting, or the date of composition.

3:1: This opening verse serves several functions. First, the combination of *mē* (anticipating a negative conclusion) with an imperative is a warning to the congregation(s) that the number of teachers should be limited. From a modern perspective, we could say that this is a form of quality control, that is, limiting the number of those who have the proper credentials and character to serve as teachers. For example, Paul lists teachers third after apostles and prophets as leaders in his churches, along with other spiritual gifts (1 Cor 12:28-30). Teachers are only one group who have received the gifts that God has given to the body of Christ (Rom 12:4-18; cf. Eph 4:11). Acts focuses on teaching as an activity carried on by the twelve and by Paul, but only once does it refer to the office or function of "teachers" (13:1) alongside that of prophets (a view developed in *Did.* xi-xv). In the Pastorals, Paul is identified as an apostle and teacher (1 Tim 2:7; 2 Tim 1:11). Other teachers are mentioned only once, with a negative connotation of leading people astray (2 Tim 4:3); but these letters emphasize adhering to the teaching of apostles as a deposit of true doctrine. James shows almost no interest in ecclesiastical offices; the only exceptions are the mention of teachers here and of elders in 5:14. In neither case does he give a job description. Normally this lack of concern for offices and organization is taken to indicate an early, fluid stage in the development of the church, even if that assumption is not always true. Second, it is obvious that James includes himself within this group, since he uses the first-person plural "we." If the author was, in fact, the brother of the Lord, then this is certainly a modest statement about his actual status in the early church. If the letter is a later composition, then it overlooks a good chance to identify James as the "first bishop of Jerusalem" or some other title that would recognize him as one of the most influential figures of the first-century church. (For a detailed discussion of the relationship of teachers and students, see Betz 1995, 619-26.)

To what extent does the reference to teachers in verse 1 control the entire section? If it were missing, we would have a collection of metaphors and examples with a broad range of applications. There is no textual support for the suggestion that 3:1-2*a* was added to an earlier document (so Dibelius and Greeven 1976, 182; Davids

1982, 135-37); and if it was added, its function in the present context is not obvious. Ralph Martin argues that the various metaphors apply primarily to Christian teachers as role models and only secondarily to other individuals. For him, "the body" refers to the church, so the teaching takes place in an ecclesiastical or even liturgical setting. The tongue is a metaphor for false teachers who have the power to lead the church astray and even to divide it (Martin 1988, 102-14). While attractive, this view reads too much into the text. While *sōma* does have corporate implications, nothing suggests that James's view of the church even approaches the Pauline image of "the body of Christ." More seriously, nothing in this letter suggests what the false teaching might be. In contrast to the Deutero-Pauline and Johannine letters, in James there is no hint of doctrinal controversies. Then what is the point of this section? The central problem emerges in verses 9-10. Cursing another human being is a sign of disrespect, and it leads directly to the kinds of controversy that we will see in 4:1-12, especially the warning against speaking evil against one another in 4:11. It looks as though squabbles threatened to divide James's congregation(s). We have already noted conflicts over the treatment of the poor and over faith and works. The message of this section, then, is that disrespect leads to divisiveness. Those who fail to control their tongues have failed an important test of Christian character.

In verse 1, James indicates that teachers will receive a "greater judgment." The phrase can refer either to the standards being applied, as the NRSV translation "with greater strictness" implies, or to the punishment for failure to meet the standards. It is not used here in a strictly eschatological sense. Anyone who has ever taught knows that evaluation and criticism are daily occurrences. However, in this verse there is also a hint of a final judgment, especially in light of 2:12 and the statement in the last part of 3:2 about achieving perfection by making no mistakes in speaking; but as usual in James it is a muted theme. In Matt 12:36-37 the same theme appears but with a much greater emphasis on the day of judgment: "You will have to give an account for every careless word you utter; for by your words you will be justified, and by your words you will be condemned."

3:2: This verse is a transition from the admonition about teachers to the speech metaphors. It begins with an aphorism that "all of us make many mistakes." The verb *ptaiō*, used twice here and once in 2:10 (where it is translated "fails") has less of a sense of moral failure than the usual verb for sinning *(hamartanō)*. As one of a series of three words stressing the letter "p," it is the first of several examples of alliteration in this section. The next clause, "anyone who makes no mistakes in speaking is perfect," deserves several comments. First, here the word for speaking is *logos*, whereas in the rest of this section (vv. 5, 6 [twice], 8) the focus shifts to the instrument of speech, the tongue *(glōssa)*. Second, the word "perfect" *(teleios)* and its cognates have appeared several times (e.g., as a description of the law in 1:25). It stood at the climax of the process of growth in 1:4, where it was translated as "mature." Here it is surprising to have speech singled out as a means of attaining perfection. The logic is that a person who has the character to control speech can control the whole body, that is, all of one's actions. That is the point of the image of the bridle, which is introduced rather abruptly in the final part of the verse (cf. 1:26). The word translated "able to" *(dynatos)* is a form of the Greek word for power *(dynamis)*. Third, we are given the impression that such self-control is, in fact, a possibility. By the time we get through the section, however, we may come back to look at this verse and wonder if it is meant ironically.

3:3-5a: There is a textual problem in verse 3 that is not serious; however, it is a perfect illustration of how hard it is to decide the best reading. Suppose you found three copies of a manuscript by a famous author. In one, the opening line reads "He is now here." Another reads "He is nowhere." The third reads "He is not here." How would you decide which is correct? The Greek manuscripts of verse 3 offer basically four readings: *ide, ei de, eide,* and *idou.* Manuscript evidence for the last two options is weaker, making them less likely. Another rule of thumb is to choose the most difficult reading, but that is not always an easy decision. In the case of *idou,* it is probable that later copyists changed the original text so that it agrees with the opening of verse 4. Most translators today (including the NRSV) adopt the second reading "if." On the other hand, *ei de* may have been changed to conform to *ei tis* at the beginning of the previous sentence in verse 2*b*, so that the reading *ide* is probably to be preferred (Mayor 1892, 101-2). If so, the sentence would begin "look," just as we often call a person's attention to something by saying "see." Fortunately, in the case of James, the meaning of the verse is not really effected.

The term "bits" in verse 3 is grammatically related to the "bridle" in verse 2, but the effect is to narrow the focus to one of the smallest parts of the apparatus. As a result, this metaphor has a double emphasis: first on the contrast in size between the small bit and the large horses, and second on the ability of the rider to make them obey or to "guide their whole bodies," a familiar theme in popular philosophy.

The same points are present in the metaphor of the boat and rudder, which follows in verse 4. The same verb for "guide" is used in both cases, creating an even stronger link between the two verses. The images of the horse and the boat are linked by a number of writers such as Plutarch and Philo (for a list of sources see, e.g., Ropes 1916, 231; or Johnson 1995b, 257-58). The opening of verse 4 is awkward (literally "Look at ships, being so large"), but this is smoothed out in most English translations. As in verse 3, the double emphasis is on the contrast in size, in this case between that of the ship and that of the rudder, and on the ability of the pilot to control the direction of the ship even under windy or stormy conditions. The alert reader can hardly miss a sharp contrast between this pilot who is in control and the doubter in 1:6 who is like a wave in a stormy sea. To suggest that the boat is the church and the rudder is the preacher (Reicke 1964, 37) is to find too specific an application for the metaphor. Instead, verse 5*a* draws a more general conclusion: although the tongue is small, it can boast of great exploits. Three of the words in this short sentence begin with the letter "m," another example of alliteration.

As noted earlier, verse 5*b* introduces a new train of thought, which continues through verse 6. It begins with *idou* ("look") just as in verse 4, although that is not clear in the NRSV. A third metaphor continues the size contrast, this time between a small fire and its ability to destroy a great forest. The term translated "forest" occurs only here in the Bible; elsewhere it can refer to firewood (Sir 28:10) or to a flame in the forest (Philo *Decal.*, 173). The adjective *hēlikos* itself implies a contrast, and so it is translated "how great" when applied to the forest and "small" when modifying the fire. There is alliteration again, also with three words, each of which has an initial aspirated sound like our "holy" and "wholly." Even though this new theme carries forward the element of contrast, what is remarkably different is the idea that the fire is destructive (cf. Isa 9:18; Ps 83:14). In other words, the notion of control is replaced by one of uncontrollable force.

3:5b-6: In case we did not get the point of the metaphor, verse 6a makes it clear: the tongue is a fire. The verb is missing, but it is best to treat it as a complete sentence, which concludes the thought of the previous verse. James did not invent this image; it is part of the Jewish wisdom tradition (e.g., Prov 16:27). In Sir 27:30–28:26 the tongue as a fire is linked with anger, remembering the commandments, avoiding conflict, and slander; only the godly will escape being burned by its flame. In James the metaphor of fire represents the tongue (Davids 1982, 141) rather than the passions, as in the Greco-Roman tradition (Dibelius and Greeven 1976, 196-98). Controlling one's speech, as a mark of Christian character, is set in the larger context of the royal law (2:8), of works as an expression of one's faith (2:14-26), of true wisdom (3:13-18), and of submission (4:7) and humility (4:10) before God.

The rest of verse 6 introduces a new metaphor of the tongue as the "world of iniquity," thus driving home the negative view that our speech causes most of our problems. The verse is extraordinarily difficult to translate, primarily because it is not clear how that phrase relates to the rest of the sentence. As a result, there have been efforts to emend the text, to find exotic meanings for some of the vocabulary, and to wrestle with the text as it stands (Davids 1982, 141-42; Baker 1995, 126-28). The term translated "iniquity" *(adikia)* can mean "injustice" or "unrighteousness" in other contexts. The word *members* is the same one that was used in verse 5a; the phrase "the whole body" has already appeared in verses 2 and

3; and the verb "placed" will appear again in 4:14. Several comments may help to make sense of a difficult passage. First, with the exception of 2:5, for James "the world" always appears in opposition to God. In 1:27, true religion is defined as keeping ourselves "pure and undefiled before God" and "unstained by the world." That demand is even clearer in 4:4, where friendship with God and with the world are presented as polar opposites. Second, in light of that understanding of the world, the fact that the tongue "stains the whole body" (v. 6) apparently makes true religion as defined in 1:27 impossible. It confirms the statement in 1:26 that if religious folk do not bridle their tongues "their religion is worthless." Third, the term "the cycle of nature" is literally "the wheel of birth," as noted by a footnote in the NRSV. That phrase has a familiar background in the ancient Orphic literature of Greece, which pictured a cycle of the birth of the cosmos, its destruction by fire, and its rebirth. By the time of James, that view had influenced Jewish thought as well as Roman popular philosophy. No exact parallel to this passage in James has been discovered, but the idea that the tongue "sets on fire" the wheel of birth certainly seems to reflect that older view. A more elaborate picture of the cycle appears elsewhere in the New Testament in 2 Pet 3:8-13. Fourth, the source of this impulse toward evil is identified. The tongue, metaphorically the world, "is itself set on fire by hell" (*Gehenna* in Greek, as the NRSV footnote indicates). The word for "set on fire" is the same in both occurrences in this verse, and in conjunction with the initial "g" of *genesis* and *gehenna* creates another example of alliteration. In the Old Testament, the Valley of Hinnom south of Jerusalem came to be viewed as an abomination, or as we would say "the pits." It was a place where trash was burned and probably a place of child sacrifice (2 Kgs 23:10; Jer 7:31; 19:5), and so it was the place where God's judgment on Israel would occur (Jer 19:1-9). In later Jewish literature, the theme of punishment is developed (e.g., *1 Enoch* 27:1-12; 2 Esd [4 Ezra] 7:36), and Gehenna is also pictured as Satan's home (e.g., *Apoc. Abr.* 14:6-8). In other New Testament passages, the image of a place of punishment predominates, especially in Matthew's Gospel; it is linked with fire in Mark 9:42-48 and Matt 5:22; 18:9.

3:7-8: Verse 7 returns to an image of taming wild animals, only to conclude in verse 8 that the tongue cannot be tamed. In these verses, James uses the verb "tame" three times in different tenses for the sake of alliteration; the only other New Testament occurrence is in the story of the Gerasene demoniac, whom nobody could tame (NRSV: "subdue") except Jesus (Mark 5:4). The image occurs in both the Jewish tradition (e.g., Ps 8:6-8; Sir 17:4) and in Roman moral thought (e.g., Seneca, *On Benefits* 2.29.4). The common thread is the sense that as human beings we are superior to other animals because we are able to tame and control them. The four classes of animals (beast, bird, reptile, sea creature) are listed in a different order from their appearance in Gen 1:26 but in agreement with Deut 4:17-18. In verse 8, after stating the conclusion that the tongue cannot be tamed, James adds that it is "a restless evil, full of deadly poison." As noted earlier, the adjective "restless" appears nowhere else in the New Testament except 1:8, although the noun is used in 3:16 where it is translated "disorder." The tongue as venomous or as an agent of death occurs in Ps 140:3 (cited in Rom 3:13; cf. Sir 5:13). In these verses, then, the important contrast is not between large and small, but between what can be tamed and what cannot. The tongue is a dangerous member of our bodies.

3:9-10: The key to this whole section, as already noted, is found in verses 9-10. The admonition here, and the earlier one in verse 1, are the only ones that do not depend directly on a metaphor for their meaning. The tongue is able to bless or to curse, which are contradictory behaviors. Interestingly enough, however, the polarity is not between blessing or cursing God, nor between blessing and cursing another human being—both of which many of us do on a regular basis—but between blessing God and cursing another person.

Blessing God suggests a liturgical setting, which is made more specific in the ascription to God as "Lord and Father." In contrast to 1:1, "Lord" clearly refers to God. The Old Testament frequently addresses God as "Lord" (e.g., Pss 31:21; 103:1). Of course, the Lord's Prayer recommends "Father" (Luke 11:2) or "Our Father" (Matt 6:9). The hymn in Rev 4:11 is praise to "our Lord and God."

Even though there is no exact parallel to the phrase "Lord and Father," it may well have been familiar in the early Jewish-Christian communities. On the other hand, the cursing, in this case, attacks those who are made "in the likeness of God," which is an obvious reference to Gen 1:27, even though the term "likeness" appears nowhere else in the New Testament. A marvelous verse in Prov 27:14 reads "Whoever blesses a neighbor with a loud voice, rising early in the morning, will be counted as cursing." Some Old Testament passages refer to cursing as something done privately (e.g., Ps 62:4), while later wisdom literature tends to be closer to James by focusing on persons who are double-tongued or, to use a more modern idiom, speaking with a forked tongue. This theme occurs in *T. Benj.* 6.5-6: "The good set of mind does not talk from both sides of its mouth: praises and curses, abuse and honor, calm and strife, hypocrisy and truth, poverty and wealth, but it has one disposition, uncontaminated and pure, toward all men. There is no duplicity in its perception or its hearing" (cf. Sir 5:14; 6:1). In later Christian writings that theme is developed in *Did.* 2:4 and *Barn.* 19:7. Verse 10 repeats the point that has just been made, that the same mouth can either bless or curse. However, the verse adds something new by condemning such behavior: "This ought not to be so." This is addressed to "my brothers," as is verse 11, so these verses are obviously an exception to the pattern where this phrase begins a new section; and it supports the argument for linking 1:16 with what precedes.

By now the central issue in the letter is emerging more clearly. The purpose of the letter is to mold Christian attitudes and behavior so that they will not be tempted to waffle in their commitment to God (1:5-8), to speak quickly and self-righteously (1:19-20), to show favoritism to the rich (2:1-4), to profess a faith that has no practical consequences (2:14-26), and yet who are quick to curse others with whom they disagree (3:9-10). This profile of "holier than thou" Christians with little compassion for others is not so much a realistic description of James's audience as it is a model of the wrong kind of behavior. It stands in sharp contrast to James's summary of the royal law with the words "You shall love your neighbor as yourself" (2:8).

3:11-12: This section concludes with four brief examples of the way in which nature is consistent, in contrast to the ambivalent behavior of human beings. Examples of a freshwater spring and of salt water bracket two examples of fruit-bearing: a fig tree and a grapevine. The point of all four illustrations is that these natural objects are incapable of producing anything different from what they were created to produce. James once again uses the device of rhetorical questions ("Does a . . . ?" and "Can a . . . ?"). Both sentences begin with a particle (*mēti* in v. 11, *mē* in v. 12), showing that the expected answer to the questions is "Of course not!" The verb "pour forth," as already noted, is unique in the New Testament, while "bitter" is used only here and in verse 14. The theme of acting according to one's nature is familiar in Stoic literature (Dibelius and Greeven 1976, 204-6 for references). In Matt 7:16-20 the saying "You will know them by their fruits" becomes an illustration for a final judgment.

◊ ◊ ◊ ◊

This section, then, focuses on a major source of divisiveness within the Christian community: indiscreet or even vindictive speech. Christian character, for teachers and all others in the community, means that we must learn how to control our speech as well as our anger, a theme already stated in 1:19-21. In 3:2*b* James assumes that this is at least a theoretical possibility. On the other hand, he seems to view the tongue as incorrigible, uncontrollable, and naturally evil (vv. 6, 8, 9-10). If that is the tongue's "nature," then is it really possible to change it? James himself seems to be ambivalent on this point. By condemning the perversion of speech in such strong terms, he seems to give the impression that there is nothing we can do to prevent it. At the same time, many of his other images and metaphors suggest that we do, in fact, have the ability to tame our speech, just as we have an obligation to express our faith in acts of justice and mercy. That is the point he wants to drive home. It is a key element in the large theme of the relationship between character and action: "Action flows from character, but character is not so much a matter of innate disposition as of training in the ways of righteousness" (Hays 1996, 99).

CHARACTER AND CONFLICT (3:13–4:12)

At first glance it is obvious that 3:13-18 deals with wisdom. What is less obvious is how these verses relate to what precedes and what follows. Generally speaking, there have been three ways of dealing that issue. The first is to treat the verses as a continuation of the previous section, primarily on the grounds that "the wise" person *(sophos)* is one of the teachers addressed in verse 1. There are some links between these sections, but verses 13-18 really introduce new material that has much more in common with what follows. Also, as I have argued, these words are spoken to the whole church and not just to a few (possibly contentious) leaders. A second solution treats this as a self-contained section with no connection to the surrounding context. At first this view looks attractive, but then we have to recognize that the section provides a smooth transition to the conflicts discussed in chapter 4. Therefore, for both stylistic and thematic reasons, it is better to adopt a third approach and treat all of 3:13–4:12 as a section dealing with the relationship between character and conflict. In it James distinguishes an earthly wisdom and its vices from a heavenly wisdom and its virtues (vv. 13-18). The former wisdom leads to disorder, the latter to peace. The next unit (4:1-6) identifies the source of conflict: our desires (v. 1; NRSV: "cravings") and our friendship with the world (v. 4). It supports this argument by appealing to the Decalogue or Ten Commandments and to other Scripture. The third unit (4:7-10) presents a plan for conflict resolution, using a series of ten aorist imperatives, implying that actions need to become habitual. The section concludes with a short but crucial unit that warns against judging one another (4:11-12). There are stylistic links, such as a series of rhetorical questions in 3:13; 4:1 (twice), 4, 5. The phrase "among you" appears in both 3:13 and 4:1, although the usual "brothers" does not appear as a transition until 4:11. There is an obvious verbal link between the word for envy *(zēlos),* which appears as a noun in 3:14, 16, and as a verb in 4:2. We will note others as we look at specific verses. Throughout this section there is an unspoken assumption: as Christians practice the appropriate virtues, both individually and collectively, they will find ways either to avoid or to resolve conflicts.

True Wisdom Produces Character (3:13-18)

The structure of this unit is fairly obvious. Verse 13 introduces it with a question directed to those in the congregation(s) who think they are wise and understanding, a group not limited to the teachers in verse 1. They are admonished to demonstrate their wisdom in practical ways by their works, presumably those that were described in 1:27 and 2:14-17. Then comes a contrast between true and false wisdom, which is really a description of two lifestyles. The negative aspect is a wisdom not from above but ultimately demonic (vv. 14-16). It is characterized primarily by envy and selfish ambition (repeated in vv. 14, 16). It leads to "disorder and wickedness of every kind," that is, to anarchy or chaos. The positive aspect is a wisdom from above (v. 17), in other words from God. As we saw in 1:5, this is the only true wisdom. It is defined by a list of virtues that is artfully constructed: a set of four beginning with the letter "e" for alliteration, followed by another set of three beginning with the letter "a." This lifestyle is peaceable, marked by an absence of "partiality or hypocrisy" (v. 17). Verse 18, which may originally have been a separate proverb, concludes the unit with a promise of "a harvest of righteousness." The words "wise" (v. 13) and "wisdom" (vv. 13, 15, 17) provide the theme for the entire unit. In addition, the terms "peaceable" (v. 17) and "peace" (v. 18, twice) describe the behavior that should characterize James's audience.

3:13-14: The unit is addressed to anyone in the community who is "wise and understanding." The combination of words is found in Deut 4:6 and Sir 21:15, and elsewhere in biblical literature along with similar terms, but this particular word for "understanding" in verse 13 *(epistēmōn)* is not found anywhere else in the New Testament. As in 2:18, the imperative "show" challenges those who think they are wise to prove it; in Greek it is actually in the third person and reads "let him show." A shift to the second person does not occur until verse 14, but the NRSV uses "you" in both verses; it also supplies the verb "are done" in verse 13, which is not in the original. The challenge is followed by three phrases that are smoothed out in most translations. Literally the verse says "Let him

97

show by good behavior his works in the meekness of wisdom." The mention of works clearly presupposes the discussion of faith and works in 2:14-26. It does not mean keeping a list of good deeds, but rather it implies developing a way of living that is infused with wisdom. The adjective "good" *(kalos)* was used in 2:17, while later in 4:17 it is translated in the NRSV as "the right thing." The noun *praütēs* is usually translated "meekness" as in 1:21, the only other occurrence in James. Matthew uses the adjectival form three times: once in the beatitude found only in Matt 5:5 and twice describing Jesus as "humble" (Matt 11:29; 21:5). Meekness or humility is a favorite virtue for James, though he prefers the verb *tapeinoō* and its cognates. We saw them in 1:9, 10. Near the end of this section they will appear again, first in the quotation from Prov 3:34 (in 4:6) and at the end of the list of virtues (4:10). This theme is therefore an important link both within this section and with 1 Peter. A striking passage in Sir 3:17-20 advises a youth to "perform your tasks *[erga]* in meekness" (RSV) and to humble himself. It was also an important theme in the community at Qumran. The term *life* is not the usual *zōē* but *anastrophē,* implying behavior or conduct. This is the only time it appears in James, although it is used in Heb 13:7 and frequently in 1 Peter. It introduces this entire section of James by drawing attention to the importance of character.

In verse 14 the particle *de* implies a strong contrast to what went before, like our "however" or "on the other hand." The words translated "bitter envy" and "selfish ambition" in the NRSV point ahead to "your cravings that are at war within you" in 4:1, strengthening the link between these two units. "Bitter" is the same word used in verse 11 to describe the "brackish" water; here it is used metaphorically. The verse contains four accusations (envy, ambition, boasting, lying), all of which will be lumped together in verse 15 as earthly wisdom, that is, as vices. Each of them is important for understanding the letter in its original setting. For example, the word for "envy" *(zēlos)* has the same root as "zealot." It is tempting, then, to see James writing to discourage Christian involvement in the violence that preceded the outbreak of the Jewish War in 66 CE, but the evidence does not really support that view. The term is much more apt to be related to general problems of dissension and conflict, like those that we see in some of Paul's churches (such as 1 Cor 14:30; 2 Cor 12:20; Gal 5:20). It is probably related to the issue of favoritism toward the rich that we saw in 2:1-13. "Ambition" could be interpreted as a desire for political office, but it is much more likely to reflect a situation within the congregation. It is paired with "envy" in verses 14 and 16 as a source of conflict. "Boasting" is another rare word, used only in 2:13 (where it is translated "triumphs over") and in Rom 11:8. There is no hint here of Paul's argument against boasting of the advantages of being Jewish and having the law (Rom 2:17-24; Phil 3:4-6). Finally, James is against being "false to the truth," or lying. As we saw in 1:19, the word of truth is a gift from God. That is why cursing another Christian (vv. 9-10) is so detestable. At the end of this section James warns against accusing a brother or sister (4:11-12), which may have the same intent as Paul's warning in 1 Cor 6:1-8 against lawsuits. Some commentators see in this passage a protest against false teaching or even a challenge to James's leadership of the church. If that was his point, it is made so subtly that it is not even stated in the text, in sharp contrast to writings like Colossians, Ephesians, the Pastoral Letters, and 2 Peter. The only possible exception in James is found in 5:19, which speaks of recovering Christians who have wandered from the truth; but that seems to mean people who have left the faith, not ones who follow the wrong leaders. We must read James for what he actually says, not in terms of controversies with "proto-Gnostics" or other false teachers found elsewhere. For James, the controversial issues concern moral behavior rather than doctrine; Christian character rather than theology.

3:15-18: The centerpiece of this unit is found in the contrast between the true wisdom that comes from God and a counterfeit wisdom (vv. 15-17). One type has already been described in terms of its negative characteristics. Those who claim to be wise but whose lives are filled with jealousy and ambition do not really have any wisdom at all. Now James reinforces that negative view by defining such wisdom as earthly, unspiritual and demonic. Usually the three terms are seen to be progressively more serious.

"Earthly" is fairly obvious. It means living according to our basic drives and instincts, living an essentially animal-like existence. "Unspiritual," on the other hand, needs some explanation. The noun *psyche*, the root of our "psychology" and related terms, often referred in Greek thought to the mental ability that distinguishes humans from other animals. In frequent New Testament occurrences, it is usually translated as "soul" or "life," as it is in 1:21 and 5:20 (the only two times in James) and thus refers to the whole person. On the other hand, the adjective "psychic" tends to have a more sinister meaning in the few times it is used. In 1 Cor 2:1-16 (especially v. 14) Paul uses it to contrast a merely human wisdom with that which is a gift of the Spirit. A contrast between the physical and the spiritual also appears in 1 Cor 15:45-46 and Jude 19. At first, Paul's view of two types of wisdom seems similar to that of James. However, James speaks about wisdom as a gift from God alone (1:15 and 3:16) and nowhere mentions the Holy Spirit. The translation "unspiritual" in this verse, then, presupposes a contrast that is never made explicit in James; the phrase "merely human" might be a more accurate translation. The third adjective in the series is "demonic," another word appearing only here in the New Testament.

In the section of the introduction dealing with James's anthropology, I distinguished two ways in which believers are asked to view their struggle with the forces of evil. From the perspective of a cosmic dualism, believers are told to focus on a few issues that are seen as matters of life or death. Such a view severely limits the scope of personal and social responsibility. The alternative, an ethical dualism, also recognizes a continuing conflict between good and evil, but it emphasizes the importance of making decisions, of affirming a value system, and of developing character. James clearly falls into the second category. For him, some lifestyles are, in fact, demonic. The marks of such a lifestyle, as stated in verse 14, are envy, ambition, boasting, and lying. They ultimately destroy personal integrity and communal relationships. In verse 16, the envy and ambition are repeated, as already noted, leading up to the result: "disorder and wickedness of every kind."

In sharp contrast the only true wisdom is "from above" (v. 17). The same word *(anōthen)* was used in 1:17 to describe God's perfect gifts; now we learn that wisdom is one of those gifts. First in the list of adjectives to describe this wisdom is "pure." It is used only here in James, but it appears in verbal form in the command to "purify your hearts" in 4:8, another link within this section. As noted above, the words translated "peaceable," "gentle," "willing to yield," and "mercy" all begin with the letter "e." The word "good" begins with the letter "a." So do the other two adjectives, in which the prefix "a-" means being "without" either partiality or hypocrisy (v. 17). Taken together, these seven virtues comprise a list of the behavior that Christians should emulate. The mention of partiality takes on special meaning in light of 2:1-7, 14-17. The praise of wisdom as a source of virtue was, of course, not invented by James. It appears frequently in Proverbs and particularly in Wis 7:22-23; 8:7. A somewhat different list of virtues is found in Gal 5:22-23 (where it is attributed to the Spirit rather than to wisdom) and in *Herm. Man.* 11.

Two words in verse 17 prepare us for the final verse in this unit. The adjective "peaceable" appears in noun form not once but twice in verse 18. The other word is "fruits," which is used again in verse 18 in the singular. There it is translated as "a harvest of righteousness" in the NRSV; the identical phrase appears in Phil 1:11. Even though this last verse may once have existed as an independent saying, it now brings the whole unit to a natural and logical conclusion. In particular, it stands over against the "disorder and wickedness" of an earthly wisdom. At the same time, there is more than one way to read verse 18. One view is that righteousness is the *condition* for making peace, which is sown *by* peacemakers (as indicated in a footnote in the NRSV). Support for this view is found in Isa 32:17: "The effect of righteousness will be peace, and the result of righteousness, quietness and trust forever." The major alternative views righteousness as the *fruit* of peacemaking, in the sense of a reward, *for* those who make peace; this is the preferred reading in the NRSV. Support for this view can be found in the Beatitudes in Matt 5:9, which promise that peacemakers will be called the children of God, and in Matt 5:10, which promise the kingdom of heaven as a reward for those who are persecuted for the sake of righteousness. Either reading of verse 18 makes peace-making a priority for Christians.

◊ ◊ ◊ ◊

The theme of this unit is that God is the source of wisdom (as in 1:15 and 1:17). The wisdom from above is what gives a person character. Throughout the unit there is a contrast between vices and virtues. The vices are earthly, unspiritual, and demonic (v. 15). They include bitter envy, selfish ambition, boasting, and lying. They produce disorder and wickedness (v. 16). The virtues include purity, peacefulness, gentleness, flexibility (willingness to yield), mercy, good fruits, and an absence of partiality or hypocrisy. The letter presents the audience with a choice of lifestyles; but for Christians, the only appropriate way to live is to be shaped by the wisdom from above.

Christians in Conflict (4:1-6)

The previous discussion of earthly wisdom has laid the foundation for this next unit, which condemns conflict in even stronger terms. Throughout the unit are a number of verbal links. The negative particle *ou* or *ouk* appears five times in the first four verses. In three places it simply means "not." Twice it introduces a rhetorical question expecting the answer "Yes": "Do they not come from your cravings?" (v. 1) and "Do you not know . . . ?" (v. 4). The nouns translated as "conflicts and disputes" in verse 1 appear as verbs in the reverse order in verse 2, forming a nice inclusion or set of bookends. The term *hēdonē*, from which we get *hedonism*, is translated as "cravings" in verse 1 and as "pleasures" in verse 3, thus forming a longer inclusion. Other themes are: asking (three times in v. 3); the two mutually exclusive types of friendship (v. 4); and God as the giver of grace (twice in v. 6). Scripture is prominent in the references to murder, coveting, and adultery, as well as in the quotations in verses 5-6.

◊ ◊ ◊ ◊

The basic issue in understanding this unit is how literally we should take James's accusations. Do the references to war, conflict, and murder reflect the actual situation of the church(es) to which he was writing, or is he speaking hypothetically and metaphorically? Do the "cravings that are at war within you" (v. 1) imply inner psychological struggles of the kind mentioned in 1:13-15, or does the phrase mean "among you" and imply physical confrontations among different members of the same congregation? The case for a literal rendering of this language hinges largely on the accusation "you murder" in verse 2. It is immediately linked with the verb *zēloō* ("you want something" in v. 2), which has the same stem as the noun used in 3:14, 16. According to some commentators, the verb should be taken literally as "don't be a Zealot"; that is, James was warning Christians not to get involved in the movement to gain Jewish independence from Roman rule. This view presupposes that the letter (or an earlier version of it) was written by James before his death in 62 CE. We cannot rule out the possibility that some Christians in Judea joined the rebels, but there is no evidence that they did. However, if the letter was directed to Jewish Christians in the Diaspora, their distance from Judea makes it unlikely that they were involved in the direct use of violence. Also, it is hard to understand why armed resistance against Rome could be explained as a result of pursuing pleasures (v. 1). Despite the harshness of this language, then, it seems better to take it symbolically, as the NRSV does when it translates *zēloute* as "you covet." At the same time, the blunt criticism means that the church(es) faced some serious problems that threatened to tear them apart. According to the author, their struggles are more than mental anguish. Their passions and their desire for pleasure are the root cause of their conflicts and may ultimately lead to overt violence.

The link between jealousy (another way to translate "zeal") and murder was familiar in the Jewish wisdom tradition (e.g., *T. Sim.* 2.6-7; *T. Dan* 1.6). Sirach 27:14-15 links swearing and pride with bloodshed, using the same word *(machē),* which appears as "disputes" in verses 1 and 2. A similar progression is seen in Jesus' antithesis in Matt 5:21-22, in which murder results from anger that can be traced back to simple disrespect for another human being. We noted a similar link with Jesus' teaching in 3:10, a condemnation of cursing. In addition to the cursing, other divisive issues may have involved the need to care for orphans and widows (1:27), along with the preferential treatment of the rich and the neglect of the poor (2:1-4, 15-16). In the present unit, then, James dramatically describes the kinds of conflict that will result unless, collectively, they can change their behavior. He does this by probing behind the behavior to the attitudes and values that support it.

4:1-3: In verse 1, the word *pothen* (from where) is repeated before both nouns, and the verb is implied rather than stated, so most translations try to be more colloquial (compare the NRSV's "Those conflicts and disputes among you, where do they come from?" with the NIV's "What causes fights and quarrels among you?"). As already noted, the term *cravings* is normally translated as "pleasures," as it is in verse 3. The only other occurrences of the word in the New Testament are in Luke 8:14 (the parable of the sower), Titus 3:3, and 2 Pet 2:13, in each case linked to other vices. The phrase "within you" is literally "in your members," reinforcing the view that the conflicts are within the congregation and not just within individuals.

Verse 2 is one of the more complicated ones in the entire letter, so if you consult other commentaries, be prepared to find ample support for quite different opinions. A literal reading, given the punctuation in the Greek text, is that found in the NIV:

> You want something but don't get it. You kill and covet, but you cannot have what you want. You quarrel and fight.

There is nothing wrong with this translation, but it seems oddly unbalanced given the skill in composition that we have come to expect from our author. An alternative solution, which takes the text as it stands but alters the punctuation slightly, is the one adopted by the translators of the NRSV.

You want something and do not have it; so you commit murder. And
you covet something and cannot obtain it; so you engage in disputes
and conflicts.

This requires adding "so" twice, even though it is not in the text;
but we will encounter other very abrupt words of address in verses
4 and 8. Also, the extra "and" at the beginning of the third line is
an unusual way to begin the next clause, and it breaks the connection between murder and coveting (i.e., zeal or envy or jealousy);
but it is not an impossible construction. The advantage of this
translation is that it dramatizes the link between our desires, our
frustration at not having them fulfilled, and the destructive actions
that happen as a result.

For some commentators a different issue in verse 2 is that the
word *kill* or *murder* seems rather extreme in relation to the other
verbs in the sentence, especially if it is not meant to be taken
literally. Erasmus suggested that instead of the word *phoneuete,*
the original text would have read *phthoneite.* The noun
phthonon actually occurs three verses later in verse 5, where it
is translated "jealousy" because of a peculiar word construction.
The substitution of this word in verse 2 would result in a pair of
words, jealousy and zeal, which are practically synonymous; they
appear together in *T. Sim.* 4.5 and elsewhere. There are two major
objections to that change. The first is that it does not appear in
any Greek manuscript. More serious is the fact that the word
murder is the same one used in the commandment "You shall not
murder" in both Exod 20:13 and Deut 5:17. The logic of the
verse in James is therefore the same as that of Matt 5:21-22: even
if you never murder anyone, but if you hate or speak to your
neighbor in a derogatory way, you are just as guilty of having
broken the law. Your attitude may lead you to do exactly what
the law forbids. Reading the text in its original form is reinforced
by the fact that, in this same unit, James cites two other commandments. At this point things get even a little more confusing.
In the Septuagint, the verb used in the commandment against
coveting is *epithymeo,* in both Exod 20:17 and Deut 5:21. The
same word is used at the beginning of this verse (4:2) in James,
but you would not know it because it is translated "You want

something" in both the NRSV and the NIV. On the other hand, the word translated "covet" in the NRSV, as we have seen, is *zēloute*, which does not appear in the Septuagint text. Thus, James combines a direct quotation with an additional allusion to the Decalogue. Furthermore, verse 4 contains a verbal citation of a different commandment, the one against committing adultery. This whole unit, then, has to be understood in light of the discussion of the law in 2:8-13. That discussion ends with a statement about judging with mercy, just as the section 3:13–4:12 will end with a warning against judging our neighbors.

Abruptly, the last part of verse 2 seems to shift gears and introduces a new topic, that of asking or prayer, which continues through verse 3. On closer inspection, though, it is not entirely new. For example, asking God was one of the first units in the letter (1:5-8), which stressed the need to ask in faith and not be double-minded. That last term will recur in the next unit in verse 8, so the two settings are very similar. In addition, the phrase that introduces this theme is "You do not have," repeating the same phrase used at the beginning of verse 2. In other words, James is now going to explain why we fail to achieve our desires. The answer falls into two parts. The first answer is that we do not receive because we do not ask. Similarly, in 1:5 those lacking in wisdom are told to ask and God will give generously. Now, because of the discussion in 3:13-18, we know what kind of wisdom is lacking: that from above. The second answer admits that we may ask, but we do not ask correctly. We ask for things that will satisfy our pleasures, which are an equivalent of earthly wisdom and its vices. There is no guarantee that we will receive whatever we ask, for God is not obligated to answer prayer. Even in 1:6-8 there is a condition, which is to ask in faith without doubting. We have already noted that the theme of doubting or double-mindedness reappears in 4:8; the theme of praying with faith will be repeated in 5:15. In these verses it is hard not to hear an echo of Jesus' sayings about asking and receiving in Matt 7:7-8 and Luke 11:9-10, except in those passages the answer to prayer seems to be unqualified, while in James it is clearly conditional.

4:4-6: Verse 4 begins confrontationally: "adulteresses." Both in form and in meaning, it is virtually synonymous with "you sinners" and "you double-minded" in verse 8. In an attempt to be more inclusive, a few ancient manuscripts added "adulterers," but that is almost certainly not the original text. Similarly, the NRSV opts for the masculine "adulterers," while the NIV broadens the term to "You adulterous people." The word is the same one used in the prohibition against adultery in Exod 20:13 and Deut 5:17 without any gender preference. The feminine form used in James reflects a biblical tradition in which the metaphor of adultery was used to describe Israel's disloyalty to the God of the covenant. It apparently originated with Hosea (especially chap 2 but also 4:12 and 9:1) and was repeated in passages such as Jer 3:20 and Ezek 16:15-52. In the New Testament, the same term appears in Jesus' sayings about an adulterous generation (Matt 12:39; 16:4; Mark 8:38) and in 2 Pet 2:14 as a condemnation of false teachers. James is not innovating, but is continuing a tradition that emphasizes the integrity of the marriage covenant by both parties. The rest of the verse introduces a different metaphor, that of friendship, which in the classical tradition was a mark of character. Here it is combined with an idea that has its roots in the biblical tradition that there are only two ways: life and death, blessing and curses (e.g., Deut 30:11-20, especially v. 19). The choice is between the God of Israel and idolatry (Josh 24:14-15). James combines the two themes in a unique way, even though he suggests that the letter's recipients should already know of this choice perhaps from what he had taught them earlier. There are only two ways to live. Friendship with the world means being an enemy of God, an idea that is repeated twice for the sake of emphasis. The alternative of being a friend of God is only implicit here, but in 2:23 Abraham was offered as a model of that kind of friendship. The "world" *(kosmos)* thus represents a mentality and a value system opposed to God, with much the same negative meaning that it has in John's Gospel. It is equivalent to the wisdom not from above that was described in 3:15. Jesus' saying about not being able to serve two masters (Matt 6:24 = Luke 16:13) contains the same kind of ethical dualism; but there it is focused on the issue of wealth, whereas for James it is a matter of one's whole life.

The rebuke in verse 4, reminding them of something obvious that they should know, is matched in verse 5 with another rhetorical question "Or do you suppose . . . ?" The argument is an appeal to Scripture, and the stated assumption is that the recipients of the letter will acknowledge its authority. The adverb translated "for nothing" is literally "emptily" or "in vain" and is not used anywhere else in the New Testament, although in adjectival form it is fairly common. There is general agreement that a colon follows "the scripture says" and what follows is a quotation. Unfortunately, the quotation bristles with difficulties, typically giving rise to a number of different solutions. The first problem is with the verb "dwell," which is transitive in some manuscripts and intransitive in others. A second problem directly related to that is the grammatical one of determining the subject of the quotation. Is it God who "yearns jealously for the spirit that he has made to dwell in us" (NRSV), or is it the spirit dwelling in us that does the yearning? Third, how is "jealously" (the word *phthonon* used in a prepositional phrase) to be understood? Nowhere else is it applied to God in a positive sense. Instead, it normally modifies human actions, like the envy and passions that have just been condemned. Thus it must be translated to convey the sense that the spirit God has put within us has jealous desires, that is, it becomes corrupt and earthly. Fourth, what is meant by the "spirit" here? Some authors see it as a reference to the Holy Spirit, but that is unlikely for two reasons. Nowhere else does James allude to the Spirit of God; rather Wisdom assumes a similar role in his thinking. More telling is the difficulty of associating jealousy with the the Spirit. The fifth problem is that no such quotation can be found in any sources known to us, biblical or otherwise. It is odd that in other places where he claims to be citing Scripture, he quotes the texts rather precisely (2:8, 11 and 4:6). James may certainly have had a more inclusive view of Scripture than we do, as did the Qumran community; but this particular quotation cannot be found in any of their sources either, nor in the hellenistic-Jewish sources that seem to have been familiar to him.

One simple solution avoids virtually all of these problems. It is to treat the punctuation after the first part of the verse as a question mark rather than a colon, thus dividing the verse into two separate questions (see especially Johnson 1995b, 280-82). The first question is therefore a general one: "Do you think that scripture speaks in vain?" It expects the response "Of course not!" The second question, then, is not a quotation from Scripture, but it does reinforce the negative view of human nature that we have seen in these last two units: "Does the spirit which he [God] caused to dwell in you have jealous desires?" The answer must be "Of course it does." In one sense it seems to divert us from the statement about having confidence in Scripture. At the same time, by reminding us of our human failures, it prepares us to hear the particular verse that James cites.

James's rebuttal in verse 6 marks the turning point from accusations to exhortations. It is, in fact, a quotation from Scripture emphasizing the promise of God. It is a literal quotation from the LXX version of Prov 3:34, except that it substitutes "God" for "Lord." Once again the "but" is emphatic. The fact that God gives grace is repeated twice, so that it brackets the statement that God opposes the proud. That theme of the reversal of fortunes, especially bringing low those who are rich, has already appeared in 1:10 and 2:5. The mention of being humble will, of course, be repeated in verse 10 as the last in the list of imperatives. The notion that God is a gracious giver reminds us of 1:5, 17. This verse from Proverbs is also cited in 1 Pet 5:5 (where the application is quite different) and in *1 Clem.* 30.2. After all of the bad news in verses 1-5, James concludes this unit with an affirmation that is both unexpected and comforting.

Christian Character and Conflict Resolution (4:7-10)

This short unit consists of only four verses, containing a list of ten moral imperatives. Yet it is the most important unit in the whole letter, for at least two reasons. First, the imperatives represent those virtues that James wants his audience to inculcate, and those actions that they need to practice in order to develop Christian character. The list is not exhaustive, but it is the very heart of James's ethical message.

Second, throughout the letter James is concerned about various kinds of conflict: within the church, with the outside world (particularly the rich who oppress them), and with evil forces that are ultimately diabolical. The values he promotes here are intended to help Christians to avoid, or at least to resolve, those conflicts at every level.

Even though it is such a short unit, the structure is intriguing. It is usually treated as a series of couplets (Davids 1982, 165), but it is really more complicated than that. The first imperative ("submit," v. 7) and the last ("humble yourselves," v. 10) are really synonymous and form an inclusion. Three of the imperatives are followed by a qualifying clause:

"Resist the devil, and he will flee from you." (v. 7)
"Draw near to God, and he will draw near to you." (v. 8)
"Humble yourselves before the Lord, and he will exalt you." (v. 10)

The first three imperatives form a nice balance: submit to God, resist the devil, draw near to God. That is followed in verse 8 by a couplet that introduces the notion of ceremonial purity ("cleanse your hands," "purify your hearts"), but reinterprets it. The verse includes two additional charges or accusations: the hearers are both sinners and double-minded. Verse 9, however, is a brief triad: "Lament and mourn and weep." The mood is quite different. Repentance is necessary. For those who have been captivated by a false wisdom and by their own passions, a different kind of reversal is needed. It is expressed in another couplet: "Let your laughter be turned into mourning and your joy into dejection." Not until verse 10 does James return to the promise of God's grace found in verse 6 in the citation of Prov 4. Here it is restated in the form of an exhortation ("humble yourselves") and a promise ("he will exalt you"). In contrast to verse 9, the reversal is a positive one. This short unit also contains some unusual vocabulary, especially in verse 9: the words "lament," "laughter," "be turned," and "dejection" are found only here in the New Testament, although a cognate of "lament" will appear in 5:1, translated as "miseries." The word for "mourning" is found nowhere else except in Revelation.

The fact that there are ten imperatives may or may not allude to the same number in the Decalogue. In any case, it is important to note that the moral reasoning here is different. These imperatives are not a set of rules or laws to be obeyed. They are not moral absolutes. James does have an appreciation for the Torah, as we have seen. Yet his perspective on the moral life has much more in common with the wisdom tradition. What he offers, therefore, are clues for developing Christian character.

◊ ◊ ◊ ◊

In verse 7, the "therefore" *(oun)* is emphatic and marks the beginning of the new unit. The verse takes several verbal cues from the scripture quotation in verse 6 and develops them in interesting ways. The prefix of the verb "submit" *(hypo)* in verse 7 is the opposite of the one used in verse 6 *(hyper)* for the "proud" who exalt themselves. Another prefix, *anti,* is part of the words *opposes* in verse 6 and *resist* in verse 7. The word *humble* in verse 6, of course, provides the theme for this entire unit, and it is repeated in verb form at the conclusion in verse 10. The first theme in this verse is to submit to God. In Heb 12:9, obedience to our natural parents is used as a reason for submitting to God's discipline. To be subject or submissive is the theme of the "household codes" (Rom 13:1-7; Eph 5:21–6:9; Col 3:12–4:1; 1 Tim 2:1-15; 6:1-2; Titus 2:2–3:2; 1 Pet 2:13–3:7), but in all of those cases the term applies to human relationships and not to our relationship to God. The second theme is to resist the devil, which has to be understood in the context of the earthly, unspiritual, and demonic wisdom of 3:15. This theme appears frequently in the *Testaments of the Twelve Patriarchs:* for example, "Observe the Lord's commandments, then, my children, and keep his law. Avoid wrath, and hate lying, in order that the Lord may dwell among you, and Beliar [the devil] may flee from you" *(T. Dan 5.1; cf. T. Naph. 8.4).* It appears later in *Herm. Man. 12,* a passage that may be dependent on James. The parallels to 1 Pet 5:5-9 are striking: a citation of the same verse from Proverbs; a call to be humble before God; and an exhortation to resist the devil, who prowls like a lion. The context in

1 Peter is different, however. It is addressed to elders and not to the whole church. Humility means that the young must accept the authority of the elders. There is no mention of the devil fleeing away. Rather, resisting the devil means that they will have to share in the suffering of Christians everywhere.%

In juxtaposition to the idea of the devil fleeing, James issues an invitation to draw near to God, with the promise that God will draw near to those who acccept the invitation (v. 8). The other imperatives in this verse (wash your hands, purify your hearts) make it clear that the imagery is drawn from the ceremonial practices of the Israelite priesthood. The priests are those who draw near to serve God (Ezek 44:15) and must wash their hands (Exod 30:17-21). Even in the Old Testament, however, "clean hands" came to be used as a metaphor for the righteous (e.g., Job 17:9; Isa 1:16). Even closer to our text is the phrase "clean hands and pure hearts" found in Ps 24:4; also Ps 73:13; cf. Sir 38:10. The image of God's drawing near in Zech 1:3 is noneschatological, as it is in James, in contrast to other images of "the coming of the Lord" or "the Day of the Lord." For James, the emphasis is on moral rather than cultic purity, as it is in Matt 5:8 and 1 Pet 1:22. It is no accident that the first adjective used to describe the wisdom from above in 3:17 was "pure." The irenic tone of verse 8 stands in sharp contrast to the epithets "you sinners" and "you double-minded." Being double-minded is the equivalent of being faithless (1:6-8), so it is the epitome of opposition to God. That is why James presents Abraham as a positive model of a person whose faith is active in love. Striking parallels to verse 8 appear in *Herm. Man.* 9.7, and in *1 Clem.* 23.1-3. The latter speaks about God bestowing his gifts of grace on those who draw near to him with a sincere mind. Then he says: "Wherefore let us not be double-minded, nor let our soul be fanciful concerning his excellent and glorious gifts. Let this Scripture be far from us in which he says 'Wretched are the double-minded, who doubt in their soul . . . '." The word *wretched* is the same rare word translated "lament" at the very beginning of verse 9, where it follows immediately the word *double-minded* in verse 8. There are so many links between these passages that we must conclude that Clement knew of and was using James as a source for his writings. It is not clear whether the word *graphē* means simply a "writing" or whether Clement regarded his source as "scripture."

Verse 9 seems out of place in a passage that is meant to give some encouragement. The normal pattern for a reversal of fortunes is the promise that those who suffer now will be comforted (so Matt 5:4) or receive an eternal reward. Our surprise is especially great when we remember 1:2: "Whenever you face trials of any kind, consider it nothing but joy." Now we are told "Let your laughter be turned into mourning and your joy into dejection." The word for "mourning," incidentally, has the same root as the verb "mourn" earlier in the sentence. In this verse, James is calling on his listeners to abandon their envy and selfish ambition (3:14) and their search for pleasures (4:1-4); in other words to repent. The picture of weeping and wailing as a sign of repentance appears in the prophetic tradition (e.g., Jer 4:8; Joel 2:12). Normally, of course, weeping and mourning are signs of grief; there is no need to look at the many examples of that behavior in the biblical tradition.

The final words in this unit do promise the kind of reversal that we were led to expect in 1:9. The condition seems simple: "Humble yourselves before the Lord." Perhaps more than any other statement in the letter this summarizes James's understanding of Christian character. To be humble means to live by the wisdom from above instead of pursuing one's own desires. It means being a friend of God and drawing near to God. The promise of more abundant grace in verse 6 is repeated, but in different words: "and he will exalt you." It is impossible to miss the similarity to the Q saying "For all who exalt themselves will be humbled, but all who humble themselves will be exalted" (Luke 18:14; also Matt 23:12). Matthew also uses the example of a child to illustrate what it means to be humble (Matt 18:4).

◊ ◊ ◊ ◊

Throughout this whole section James moves back and forth between two poles. He begins in 3:13 by talking about our good life when our works are done with gentleness born of wisdom. Then he shifts and condemns a way of living apart from that wisdom, only to return to a positive description of the wisdom that is a gift from above. He ends with an appeal for making peace. Suddenly, he shifts back to describe, in graphic terms, the reasons for the conflicts that arise not just in the world but even in the church. Following that rather hostile attack on his listeners, he uses a quotation from Scripture to return to a positive vision of the Christian life. He lists those values by which he expects Christians to live. The last and most important of those is humility, which brings us back to the note of gentleness in 3:13 and of making peace in 3:18. That would seem to be a good place to end this section. In fact, not many commentators find a direct connection with the verses that follow. However, I am convinced that there is one, so let us turn to the final unit in this section and see what we can discover.

Christian Morality: Speaking and Judging (4:11-12)

The mention of "brothers," the first in a long time, marks the beginning of a new unit. It is certainly possible to see this unit as the start of a section that continues through 5:6, although the links are not very apparent. An alternative is to see it as a self-contained unit. Structurally, the two verses are extremely dense. The word meaning to "speak evil against" ("evil" is implied, not stated) occurs three times. So does "brother(s)." The verb for "judging" occurs four times, and the noun "judge" twice. "Law" appears four times, always without a definite article, and "lawgiver" once (the only New Testament occurrence). The content thus picks up three themes that we have seen earlier, and condenses them into one passage: proper speech (1:19-20, 26; 3:1-12); the law (1:22-25; 2:8-12); and judgment (2:13). The strongest argument for linking this unit with what precedes is a structural parallel to 2:8-13. There the discussion of the law, which focused on love for the neighbor (2:8), ended with a warning about being judged by the law of liberty (2:12-13). The present section has already included a discussion of the law in 4:1-4 and now draws to a close with a warning against judging one's neighbor (4:12). Also, in the early part of this section there was a warning against being false to the truth, that is, lying (3:14). Now that theme is repeated with the stern

warning against speaking evil against another Christian. So ends
the section dealing with conflict inside the community.

◊　◊　◊　◊

The address to the "brothers" is a way of putting James's message
on a more personal basis after the tirade in the earlier part of this
section. The meaning of speaking against one's neighbor is not
entirely clear. Does this mean giving false witness, thus violating
another commandment? Or does it imply slander and spreading
rumors? There is Old Testament precedent in Pss 49:20 and 101:5
and in other passages such as Wis 1:11. Even more striking is Lev
19:16, where the warning against slander occurs in the same
context as the saying about love for one's neighbor (Johnson 1982,
395). The strongest support for this view comes from New Testament vice lists (Rom 1:30; 2 Cor 12:20; 1 Pet 2:1; cf. 1 Pet 2:12
and 3:16, which refer to outsiders who malign the Christians). It is
also supported by the later tradition in *Herm. Man.* 2.3. In *1 Clem.*
30.3 the same term occurs in conjunction with a citation of Prov
3:34 and a saying about being justified by works rather than words,
another fairly obvious reference to James. Of course, the warning
against slander must be read in light of the advice in earlier
passages: about being slow to speak (1:19-20); about bridling one's
tongue (1:26); and especially the stern warning against cursing
another Christian (3:9-10).

Verse 11 contains three separate sentences. The first is simply a
command not to slander one another. The second expands the
prohibition to include both slander and judging one another. In a
parallel construction, it explains that whoever slanders or judges
another person also slanders and judges the law. The missing
premise is found earlier in 2:8, which cites the commandment
"You shall love your neighbor as yourself." The conclusion here
is that an action taken against another Christian violates the law
itself. The third sentence makes that point even clearer. It begins
"but if you judge the law." Notice the progression that has just
taken place: slandering a brother; slandering or judging a
brother; slandering or judging the law; judging the law. What are
the consequences? First, if you do this, you are not a doer of the

law. This statement must be understood in light of the exhortation in 1:22-25 to be doers of the word and the law of liberty, and also in light of the warning in 2:10: "For whoever keeps the whole law but fails in one point has become accountable for all of it." A few manuscripts try to soften the force of "not a doer of the law" by substituting "no longer" *(ouketi)* for "not" *(ouk)*. The second consequence is that you have put yourself above the law. Rather than hearing it and obeying it, you have become a judge. This contradicts the advice given in 2:12: "So speak and so act as those who are to be judged by the law of liberty."

To put yourself above the law is to put yourself in God's place, as verse 12 quickly points out. There is only one lawgiver and one judge, both images of God that are deeply rooted in the biblical tradition. The statement that God "is able to save and to destroy" prepares us for the judgment scene in 5:7-9. The last sentence in this unit is almost anticlimactic, since its purpose is to reinforce the points made in verse 11. There is an important verbal shift, however, from "brother" in verse 11 to "neighbor." The reference to 2:8, the love commandment, is now explicit. This long section dealing with conflict in the Christian community ends, then, with a note of judgment, just as the earlier section did in 2:13: "For judgment will be without mercy to anyone who has shown no mercy; mercy triumphs over judgment."

In this long section James has dealt with conflict from several points of view. The first unit (3:13-18) focuses on wisdom from above as an essential ingredient in developing character. James identifies those vices that lead to conflict, and he praises those virtues that help to create peace. The second unit (4:1-6) locates the source of conflict in our desire for those things that we do not have, not in demonic powers that have control over us. To have character is to take responsibility for our actions. Ultimately, we are faced with a choice between two different lifestyles, friendship with the world and friendship with God. James views them as fundamentally incompatible. In that context, the third section (4:7-10) spells out those virtues that Christians should cultivate. Finally, the section concludes with a warning against judging one another (4:12-13). More than any other section in the letter, this one condenses the author's view of Christian morality and Christian character.

CHARACTER AND WEALTH (4:13–5:6)

This is a well-defined section in two parts, each beginning with the same challenge: "Come now" (4:13 and 5:1). It consists of a general moral condemnation of the rich. Those who are being criticized are apparently wealthy outsiders and not church members, although some Christians might still identify with the criticisms. The section lacks any mention of "brothers," unlike the end of the preceding unit (4:11) and the beginning of the next section (5:7; also in 5:12, 19).

The style of this section, particularly in the second unit, is that of a prophetic denunciation, for example like that of Amos: "Hear this, you that trample on the needy, and bring to ruin the poor of the land" (8:4; cf. 2:6-8). Keep in mind, however, that a special concern for widows and orphans and the poor was also ingrained in the Torah, as we saw in 1:27. It is maintained in the wisdom tradition as well. For example, Wis 1:16–2:11 satirizes the words of the ungodly who live only for today, who oppress the defenseless, and for whom might makes right; see especially 2:10: "Let us oppress the righteous poor man; let us not spare the widow or regard the gray hairs of the aged."

Once again there are a large number of rare words. Those occurring only in this passage are: "wail" (5:1); "rotted" and "moth-eaten" (5:2); "rusted" (5:3); "mowed," "kept back," "cries" (5:4); "lived . . . in luxury" (5:5). Several others occur only one or two other times in the New Testament: "doing business" (4:13); "mist" and "vanishes" (4:14); "arrogance" (4:16); "miseries" (5:1); "rust" (5:3); "lived . . . in pleasure" and "slaughter" (5:5); "condemned" (5:6). A surprising number of them are used by *1 Clem.*: arrogance in 21.5; misery in 15:6; rot in 25:3; and slaughter in 16.7 (citing Isa 53). Some of these words are attracted to each other by the theme, such as the mist that vanishes. At the same time, within such a short section of the letter there is a remarkably rich vocabulary.

The first unit (4:13-17) condemns the acquisition of wealth, primarily by traveling merchants, while the second unit (5:1-6) demonstrates the worthlessness of wealth, primarily that of large landowners (Maynard-Reid 1987, 68-98). The theme therefore resumes the discussion of the rich and the poor from 1:9-11 and 2:5-7. In both units James shows why a preoccupation with wealth is a character flaw. Without referring directly to earlier passages, he shows how such a person lacks the maturity and completeness that God expects (1:4) and has instead become friends with the world (4:4). The condemnation of wealth provides a counterpoint to the poverty of the Christians. Their situation and that of the rich who oppress them stand in sharp contrast to each other, a point driven home at the beginning of the following section (5:7-11).

Character and the Search for Wealth (4:13-17)

The structure of this first unit is quite simple. Verses 13-15 contrast two attitudes on the part of the traveling merchants. James condemns those who think that they can control their own lives without any reference to God, but he recommends that they make their plans in light of God's will for them. Each of these attitudes is given in the form of a quotation, the first one put into the mouths of the merchants (v. 13) and the second in the form of advice from the author (v. 15). Their main character flaw is summarized as arrogance (v. 16). The final verse is probably an independent saying, indicated in part by the shift from second to third person. It is only loosely related to the rest of this unit, even though it does recall the discussions of doing the word (1:22-25) and faith without works (2:14-26). We have noted similar loosely connected sayings in 2:13 and 3:18.

In addition to the pair of questions, there are other links within the section. The emphatic "now" *(nun)* in verse 13 appears in a different construction in verse 16 *(nun de)*, where it signifies a sharp contrast. Literally it means "but now," as in the GNB. "As it is" in the NRSV and NIV softens the tone. In verse 13 three of the Greek words begin with the letter "p," giving us assimilation that cannot be conveyed in English. In verse 13, the words "we will go" *(poreusometha)* and "doing business" *(emporeusometha)* are identical except that the latter has a prefix. The repetition of "tomorrow" helps tie together verses 13 and 14. "Boasting" appears twice in verse 16, once as a noun and once as a verb. The verb *poieō* is translated as "spend (a year)" in verse 13 and as "do" in verse 15, and it appears twice in verse 17 in different forms.

◊ ◊ ◊ ◊

Throughout this unit there are a number of textual issues. None of them is serious, and the NRSV translation follows the best options in each case. For example, in verse 13 some manuscripts read "today and tomorrow" instead of "today or tomorrow" and want to limit the sojourn to one year. The verbs are correctly translated in the future tense ("we will go," etc.) and not as "let us go." The text of verse 14 has several variants, including the insertion of a definite article before "tomorrow" and of the word "for" after the word "what." One way of reading the verse is to take the entire first half as an indicative statement, as in the Jerusalem Bible: "You never know what will happen tomorrow." The NRSV and NIV correctly divide the sentence, with the second clause read as a question: "What is your life?" In the answer, that "you are a mist that appears for a little while and then vanishes," the two verbs both contain the "ph" sound, giving us another example of assonance. Verse 15 begins with an infinitive construction rather than an imperative, but the translation "instead you ought to say" conveys the sense of the phrase. Similarly, in the phrase "if the Lord wishes," the verb is in the subjunctive in some manuscripts and in the present tense in others, but there is no significant difference in the meaning. The theme of traveling, which began in verse 13, now comes to an end. In verse 16, James explains the rationale behind his criticism of the merchants. They have the wrong attitude, one of boasting in their ability to control their own lives. Some manuscripts use a different but related verb for "boasting" (the one used in 2:13 and 3:14) without any important change in meaning. The rare word for "arrogance" is used only in 1 John 2:16 and later in *1 Clem.* 21:5. James's definition of sin is introduced in verse 17 by an emphatic "therefore," watered down as "then" in the NRSV. The conclusion, introduced by *oun* (better translated as "therefore" than simply "then"), is that sin is not a failure of knowing but a failure to act. That conclusion is consistent with the basic message of the letter, but it does seem to shift the focus away from the wrong attitude (arrogance) to action (or in this case a failure to act on what we already know to be moral).

◊ ◊ ◊ ◊

The merchants' character flaw is described in three different, but related, ways. First of all, it is boasting, the presumption that we are in complete control of our own lives and do not need God. It is the attitude that characterizes secularism in its various forms. We have already seen what it is like in 3:14, where boasting is linked with bitter envy, selfish ambition, and being false to the truth. The only kind of boasting that is permitted, according to James, is that of the humble person who boasts in being raised up by God (1:9). The contrast of attitudes could hardly be clearer.

The second term that describes the flawed attitude is arrogance, which is linked with boasting in verse 16. In James's description of these merchants planning their buying expeditions it is hard not to think of Jesus' saying "For what will it profit them to gain the whole world and forfeit their life?" (Mark 8:36; cf. Matt 16:26 and Luke 9:25). The parallel is made even sharper by the question "What is your life?" followed by the description of it vanishing like mist. Their death does not occur in some apocalyptic disaster. Rather, they simply fade away. The mood is almost identical to that of 1:10-11, where it also applies to the fate of the rich. In *1 Enoch* 97:8-10 and 4 Ezra 7:61 the image of mist or smoke appears, but in an apocalyptic context.

Third, James characterizes their flaw as sin (v. 17). The definition of sin is knowing the right (literally "good") thing to do and failing to do it. We have noted praise for Christians who do well (2:8, 19) and whose good life demonstrates a gentleness born of wisdom (3:13), in contrast to those Christians in 2:14-26 whose faith does not produce good works. This definition of sin seems to shift the argument from the merchants' attitude to their failure to act, but it is not a matter of either/or. The assumption is that they know the will of God and fail to do it, but that clearly is not the case. Because of their boasting and their arrogance, the merchants have failed to learn the will of God. This is made clear in the saying "If the Lord wishes" in verse 15, an assumption they do not acknowledge. There is no known source of the quotation, which many scholars refer to as the *conditio Jacobaea*. However, there are frequent references to the will of God in the New Testament: for example, "Whoever does the will of God is my brother and sister and mother" (Mark 3:35; cf. Matt 12:50) and the Lord's Prayer (Matt 6:10). The most frequent references in Jesus' teaching are found in Matthew, who usually speaks of it as the will of the "Father" (Matt 7:21; 12:50; 18:14; 21:31). Similar references are found in John, Luke–Acts, Paul's letters, Hebrews, and in 1 Pet 3:17. The merchants fail, then, on two counts. They do not know the will of God, and so they fail to do it. Their lifestyle is the opposite of true religion as defined in 1:27.

Character and the Possession of Wealth (5:1-6)

This unit is a prophetic oracle in the form of an indictment. In the Old Testament, such an indictment is sometimes used against Israel (as in Hos 4:1-19; Amos 2:4-16), but it may also call other nations to be accountable (e.g., Amos 1:2–2:3; Isa 41:21-29). Although he does not claim to speak directly for God, James presents a list of charges against the wealthy landowners who are apparently outside the community of faith; and he predicts that their judgment is assured. We may even imagine a courtroom setting. Within this setting, verse 1 resembles a dirge or lament. It calls on the rich to "weep and wail at miseries that are coming to you." The word for wailing is *ololyzontes;* like our "ululate," it is especially onomatopoetic. In tone, if not in form, this unit is similar to Luke 6:24: "But woe to you who are rich, for you have received your consolation."

Like the previous unit, this one begins with "come now" and condemns a class of prominent people. However, there are two important differences here. One is that the criticism is unrelenting. It repudiates the rich, not because of their attitude, but just because they are rich. The other is the strong apocalyptic element here, introduced by the mention of the last days in verse 3. Rather than fading away like mist, these rich people will be destroyed by fire (v. 3). They have prepared themselves to be slaughtered (v. 5).

The structure of the unit is simple. The opening verse calls the rich to grieve. This is not a call to repentance; apparently it is too late for that. Then the four charges in the indictment are presented (Martin 1988, 176-84). Their wealth is worthless (vv. 2-3). They have cheated their workers by withholding wages due to them (v. 4). They are greedy and love their luxury (v. 5). Finally, they have murdered the righteous one, who was presumably both poor and innocent, and who did not resist. The character of the victim thus underlines the seriousness of the charges against the rich and powerful.

The only verbal link within the unit is the word for "you rich people" (v. 1), which is related to the term for their wealth (v. 2). However, there are several interesting links to 4:6-10. The word for miseries (v. 1) is related to the verb that was translated as "lament" in 4:9. Similarly, the word *weep* in verse 1 was also used in 4:9. The most interesting link comes at the very end of this unit. The word *resist* (v. 6) is the same one that we saw in the quotation from Ps 3:34 in 4:6. There it was translated "opposes." The quotation ("God opposes the proud, but gives grace to the humble") provides an appropriate context for understanding the current section. We have seen the opposition to the proud beginning in 4:13 and reaching a climax in the murder charge of verse 6. By contrast, God's grace to the humble will be the theme of verses 7-11.

◊ ◊ ◊ ◊

There are not many textual variants within this unit. One, which is not well attested, would change "those who weep" in verse 1 from second- to third-person plural. Another inserts "rust" again in verse 3 to make it clear that it is the subject of "will eat your flesh." The phrase "kept back" in verse 4 has alternate readings, but this is the best option. Some manuscripts insert "as" before "in the day of slaughter" (v. 5), but that weakens the sense within the unit that there is no escape. Finally, some interpreters take the final clause about the righteous man's nonresistance as though it were a question, but in view of the other strong assertions in this passage, it seems like a weak conclusion.

Our look at the text will proceed in two stages. First we will follow the flow of the argument as James presents it in this unit, looking at other texts that represent a similar way of picturing the world. Then we will come back and look at the unit from the viewpoint of its inner logic.

5:1-3: As noted earlier, the opening verse includes an unusual reference to wailing, a verb used only here in the New Testament, although it occurs nineteen times in the Old Testament (LXX), always in the prophetic tradition. It is usually associated with calamities or with the impending Day of the Lord, as in Isa 13:6: "Wail, for the day of the LORD is near; it will come like destruction from the Almighty!" While that "day" is not mentioned in James, the image of a final judgment is clear in this passage, and it becomes even more explicit in the next section (vv. 8-9).

The first charge against the rich is that their wealth is corrupt; it cannot last. Here again we make contact with a Q saying of Jesus (Matt 6:19-21 = Luke 12:33-34). What those Gospels have in common is the summary saying "For where your treasure is, there your heart will be also." In another respect, they are quite different. Matthew's version warns against laying up treasures on earth. Rather than accumulate wealth, lay up your treasure in heaven. Luke's version focuses much more on the use of that wealth: "Sell your possessions, and give alms" (12:33). It occurs in the context of a series of pericopes that warn against accumulating wealth and advise readers how to use it (Luke 12:13-34). As usual, James is much closer to the Matthean version. His attack on the rich is more concerned with the possession of wealth than with its use, although we know from 1:27 and 2:15-16 that both are important to him.

The "miseries" are spelled out in verses 2-3 in three statements: (a) your riches have rotted; (b) your clothes are moth-eaten; and (c) your gold and silver have rusted. The verbs are in the perfect tense, but they are anticipatory. Thus the process of decay is already under way. Realistically, James is not claiming that the rich have already suffered the loss of everything they own. Rather, this is a dramatic way of saying that all of these things are worthless and doomed for destruction. Gold and silver, of course, do not rust; James is suggesting that even such valuable metals will not survive. A similar idea is found in Ezek 7:19, where silver and gold cannot save the sellers. The worst is yet to come, however, for the rust (not the same word as the verb in v. 2) will consume their flesh like fire! In the Old Testament, fire is often associated with God's judgment, usually against foreign nations (e.g., Isa 30:27-28; Amos 1:12-14), but only in the Apocryphal book of Judith (16:7) is it said to consume flesh. In the section of 1 Enoch that pictures conflict between the righteous and sinners (Book V, 91-104), we read "Those who amass gold and silver, they shall be quickly destroyed. Woe unto you, O rich people! For you have put your trust in wealth" (94:7-8). Later we read that those who oppress the righteous will burn in "blazing flames worse than fire" (11:7-9). The idea that sinners will be destroyed by fire is also found in Rev 11:5 and 20:9. In James the eschatological imagery is brief but gruesome.

What have the rich done to deserve such a fate? They have "laid up treasure in the last days" (v. 3). Reading "in" rather than "for" the last days (against the NRSV) is more consistent with the perfect tense of the verbs, that is, with the idea that destruction has already begun. It is also more consistent with the impending fire (v. 3) and slaughter (v. 5). Thus the NIV reads verse 3c as "You have hoarded wealth in the last days." A similar theme is found in material peculiar to Luke. The first is a saying "Take care! Be on your guard against all kinds of greed; for one's life does not consist in the abundance of possessions" (Luke 12:15). This is followed immediately by a parable about a man who decides to build bigger and bigger barns only to discover that he will die that very night (12:16-20). The figure of the wealthy landowner was apparently a ready target in early Christian rhetoric. The parable is then followed by another saying on the same theme: "So it is with those who store up treasures for themselves but are not rich toward God" (12:21). Luke goes on to record further instruction by Jesus (from Q) about possessions, ending with a verse that parallels James's concern for single-minded devotion to God: "For where your treasure is, there your heart will be also" (12:34).

5:4: The second charge, introduced with the attention-getting "Listen!" *(idou),* is that the owners have refused to pay their workers the wages due them. The context for this charge appears explicitly in Deut 24:14-15.

> You shall not withhold the wages of poor and needy laborers, whether other Israelites or aliens who reside in your land in one of your towns. You shall pay them their wages daily before sunset, because they are poor and their livelihood depends on them; otherwise they might cry to the LORD against you, and you would incur guilt.

It also appears in Lev 19:13: "You shall not defraud your neighbor; you shall not steal; and you shall not keep for yourself the wages of a laborer until morning." This verse occurs in the same passage with the commandment about loving your neighbor (Johnson 1982, 394). Sirach 34:26 is less specific about the laborer but more specific about the violation of the law: "To take away a neighbor's living is to commit murder; to deprive an employee of wages is to shed blood." All of these verses and similar ones tell us a great deal about the risks of being a farmworker in Israel. For the first Christian century, information comes from several sources. In the synoptic Gospels, many of Jesus' sayings and parables assume an agricultural environment. Particularly relevant to the situation of hired hands are his parables of the unforgiving servant (Matt 18:23-25), the prodigal son (Luke 15:11-32), the laborers in the vineyard (Matt 20:1-16), and the wicked tenants (Matt 21:33-46; Mark 12:1-12; Luke 20:9-19).

For the situation in Galilee before the outbreak of the Jewish revolt, our best source is Josephus, the Pharisee who was made general in order to recruit troops in that province for the Jewish resistance, but who ultimately surrendered to Vespasian and became a favorite of the Flavian emperors. In his *Antiquities* and particularly in *The Jewish War,* he describes the tension between the cities, which were predominantly hellenistic, and the rural towns (see also Freyne 1980, Horsley 1995). Most of the population, probably 90 percent, lived close to the land, either on family farms or in small villages. In many cases, the family property had been expropriated by the Hasmonean rulers, by their successors the Herodians, by the Romans, or by lenders who foreclosed on loans and took the land. During the period of Jesus' ministry and the time before the Jewish War, those who owned their own farms were forced to pay tribute to the Romans (under Herod Antipas as much as 25 percent of their income every other year). They were also forced to pay taxes to the tetrarch (or ethnarch) Herod Antipas for his aggressive building program (cities such as Sepphoris and Tiberias). In addition, they were expected to pay a tithe to the temple for support of the priesthood. Those who lost their property through foreclosure became hired hands of the wealthy, absentee landlords. Galilee was a peasant culture that had to support the lavish lifestyle of the minority ruling class. That is exactly the situation being described by James, although it was certainly not limited to Galilee.

Another source is the Mishnah. It records the interpretation of Torah by Pharisees who were contemporaries of the early Christians and by the early rabbis who assumed the direction and leadership of Judaism after the fall of Jerusalem. The entire first section of the Mishnah is devoted to interpreting regulations in the Torah having to do with agriculture (*Zeraim* or "seeds"). Some of the debates concern what a field hand may pick and eat, or take home to replant. It is not always clear which issues apply to the years before the Jewish revolt, the period of Jesus' ministry and perhaps of the composition of the epistle; but the general picture is almost certainly relevant.

Three aspects of verse 4 deserve some comment. First, withholding wages is a direct violation of the Torah, even if the rich who are being accused do not accept that law as a basis for defining their character and their behavior. James is drawing on prophetic denunciations like Jer 22:13: "Woe to him who builds his house by unrighteousness, and his upper rooms by injustice; who makes his neighbors work for nothing, and does not give them their wages."

Malachi 3:5 has a list of invectives, including ones against "those who swear falsely, against those who oppress the hired workers in their wages, the widow and the orphan, against those who thrust aside the alien, and do not fear me, says the LORD of hosts." In this passage, James clearly stands in that prophetic tradition. Second, the phrase "the Lord of hosts" is also used in this verse in James. In Hebrew the words "Yahweh Sabaoth" symbolize God as the commander in chief of an angelic or cosmic army, capable of defeating all forces of evil (Sleeper 1996, 85-99, with footnotes and bibliography). In this verse "Lord" refers to God and not to Christ.

5:5: As already noted, the rich are condemned primarily for their accumulation of wealth and their ostentatious lifestyle, rather than for their failure to give to the poor. That is also the point of verse 5. A lack of charity is no doubt implicit, but it is not the main point that James is making. Similarly, the image of a rich person who is oblivious to the needs of the beggar Lazarus appears in Jesus' story in Luke 16:19-31, where the theme is the reversal of fortunes of the rich and the poor. The connection of a day of slaughter with darkness and divine judgment is found in *1 Enoch* 84:8-9. In James, that connection is not actually stated in this verse, but preparation for the "day of slaughter" is closely linked to the imminence of the divine judge in 5:9. In the Hebrew Bible, the image is almost always linked with the slaughter of lambs; in Ps 44:11, 22 it refers to the Israelite exiles. However, Jer 25:30-38, especially verse 34, portrays God's judgment against the nations; they are the shepherds who will be slaughtered. The passage that sheds the most light on James is also found in Jeremiah, where he is dealing with the question of theodicy. The prophet challenges God to deal with those who are guilty and treacherous and yet who prosper: "Pull them out like sheep for the slaughter, and set them apart for the day of slaughter" (12:3). The sentiment is similar to that of James, who asserts that the rich have been fattening themselves (their "hearts" as well as their bodies) for that day.

5:6: The most serious charge is found here in verse 6. It accuses the rich of having "condemned and murdered the righteous one, who does not resist you." We already noted the saying in Sir 34:22 that to deprive a worker of wages is the equivalent of murdering him. James may be making the same point, but once again it is not clear that he is doing so. Most of the speculation about this verse has been the identity of "the righteous one." If it refers to an individual, who is that person? It is no surprise that some interpreters (e.g., André Feuillet) see here a reference to Jesus Christ, particularly in light of Isa 53:7 ("like a lamb that is led to the slaughter, and like a sheep that before its shearers is silent, so he did not open his mouth"). There are several problems with this interpretation. First, nowhere else is the death of Jesus attributed specifically to those who are rich. Second, in the previous verse in James, it is the rich who are being prepared for slaughter, not Jesus. Third, there is no indication that James is referring to the verse in Isaiah, in sharp contrast to 1 Pet 2:23, which develops an extended soteriological argument based on Isa 53. Fourth, and perhaps most important, in the New Testament many other figures are described as being righteous (e.g., Joseph in Matt 1:19; Zechariah and Elizabeth in Luke 1:6; Simeon in Luke 2:25; Abel in Matt 23:35, which explicitly refers to other prophets who were murdered). Only in 1 John 2:1 does "Jesus Christ the righteous" appear in anything like a title. An alternative, especially if James was written by a later anonymous author, is that "the righteous" refers to James himself. Keep in mind, as we saw in the introduction, that this was a designation used for him in the early church. Even if it could be proven that the letter was written by the Lord's brother, the circumstances of his death and the appellation "the righteous one" would have been understood as "a tribute paid to the historical James" (Martin 1988, 182). It is much more likely, however, that the term does not refer to an individual. Rather, it includes those Christian peasants who were poor and oppressed, who refused to participate in armed violence, but who instead accepted their deaths at the hands of the wealthy and powerful. A possible context for this verse is the Q saying that condemns Jerusalem for killing the prophets (Matt

23:37-39 = Luke 13:34-35), which in Q almost certainly includes the early Christian prophets. For James, the rich landowners are not identified with Jerusalem; but their treatment of the "righteous" is just as ruthless.

◊ ◊ ◊ ◊

At the conclusion of the unit dealing with the merchants, we saw how James views the character flaw of the rich (their failure to acknowledge God's lordship and will) and their sin (failure to act on what they know to be the right/good thing to do). Now we need to analyze the moral argument that he uses in his condemnation of the rich landowners. We can best do that by asking four questions that will help us to get at the reasoning behind his accusations.

"What have the rich done?" For one thing, they have "laid up treasure" (v. 3), a charge that is reinforced by saying that they have lived "in luxury and in pleasure" (v. 5). In violation of Jesus' own teaching, even though that is not quoted directly, they have pursued the accumulation of earthly wealth. Moreover, they have withheld wages legitimately earned by their workers, in violation of God's will spelled out in the Jewish tradition (v. 4). Most serious of all, they have condemned and killed the righteous one (v. 6). Thus the basic four charges can be reduced to three, since verses 3 and 5 are essentially the same.

If metaphorically this is a judicial proceeding, then the second question has to be "What is the evidence against the rich?" Two major pieces of evidence are offered: the rust that is the residue of the corrupt wealth they had accumulated (v. 3), and the cries of the workers who had been cheated out of their income (v. 4). God has heard those cries, so in effect the judge has already heard from the plaintiffs and is prepared to decide for them.

If that is true, then the next obvious question is "What happens to the rich as a result?" One answer is that the accumulation of wealth amounts to nothing. Their possessions, clothes, and even valuable coins and jewelry have already lost their value (v. 3). The rich are essentially bankrupt. The other answers are even less appealing. Their flesh will be burned (v. 3) and they will be slaughtered (v. 5).

Finally, "When does this happen?" James suggests that the process is already at work (v. 3). They are living in the last days. In effect, this is a partially realized eschatology. Nevertheless, the climax (the day of slaughter) is still in the future. That is when the rich will finally be brought low. It is also, as we will see in the next unit, the time when the faithful and just will be raised up.

CHRISTIAN CHARACTER AND CHRISTIAN COMMUNITY (5:7-20)

This section (5:7-20) brings the letter to a close. It consists of two units. The first (vv. 7-11) reminds the readers or listeners of the need for patience in the time remaining before Christ's *parousia*. In other words, it deals with the attitude and conduct of individual Christians. Thus it returns to one of the opening themes of the letter (1:2-4, 12). The second unit (vv. 12-20) is more concerned with interrelationships within the Christian community. Three separate issues are addressed. It certainly would be possible to treat them as discrete units, but to do so would miss the overall picture of community life that James portrays in this closing portion of the letter. One issue (v. 12) concerns oath taking, thus approaching from a different angle the question of appropriate speech (1:19-20, 26; cf. 2:12; 3:1-12; 4:11-12). A second theme (vv. 13-18) is prayer, which was introduced in 1:5-8 and was discussed again in 4:2-3. Here prayer is linked to the problems of illness and the forgiveness of sins. Finally, verses 19-20 exhort Christians to rescue those who have left the faith, thus strengthening the community (cf. 1:3-4, which also deals with the need to become stronger in faith). Every passage within this section thus refers back to a theme in the opening chapter, forming an inclusion as well as a conclusion.

The entire section, then, is a collection of pieces of advice on several different topics. There are not many verbal connections between the units. "Brothers" is repeated (vv. 7, 9, 10, 12, 19; the NRSV uses "beloved" and "brothers and sisters") to get attention and also to provide reassurance. "The Lord" is used five times in the first unit (vv. 7, 8, 10, 11 [twice]) and again in verses 14-15. The unusual word for "suffering" in verse 10 *(kakopathia)* is used as a verb in verse 13.

As usual, there are some rare words. Those used only here include: "the early (rain) and the late (rain)" in verse 7; "suffering" (v. 10, though in verb form in v. 13); "compassionate" (v. 11). Others are used fewer than five times elsewhere in the New Testament: "call blessed" (v. 11); "cheerful" (v. 13); "prayer" *(euchē)* and "the sick" (v. 15); "a human being like us" (v. 17); and "yielded" its harvest (v. 18).

What really ties the units together, however, is a concern for Christian character within the context of the community of faith. James is reminding his audience once again of the attitudes and behavior that are the marks of the Christian life, both individually and collectively. Moreover, he talks explicitly about the responsibility that they should exercise toward one another, including those who apparently have left the congregation.

◊ ◊ ◊ ◊

Personal Character in a Time of Crisis (5:7-11)

In many respects this unit is a mirror image of verses 1-6. Both mention "the Lord" prominently. Both refer to an eschatological judgment. Both use agricultural analogies to make their main point. The word *idou*, translated "Listen!" in verse 4, occurs three times in this unit (vv. 7, 9, 11) although most English translations do not make that clear. However, two things indicate that verse 7 begins a new section. One is the shift of audience from the rich to members of the community ("brothers"), a shift that is maintained through the end of the letter. The other is the emphatic "therefore" *(oun)*. As we have seen on other occasions, it marks a transition. In this passage, Christian morality is shaped by their situation (their poverty) and by their theology (their knowledge that God will execute justice for them).

The unit is incredibly dense. The main theme is captured by two Greek roots: be patient (twice in v. 7, again in v. 8, and as a noun in v. 10) and endure (in two different forms in v. 11). The coming *(parousia)* of the Lord is mentioned in verses 7 and 8, the only references in James. As noted above, *idou* and "brothers" are each used three times and "the Lord" five times.

There are several textual variants, but few of them change the meaning of the text significantly. Some versions add "rain" a second time to make explicit what is implied in the "early and late" rains. A few add the word "fruit" after "receives" in the last part of verse 7, thus implying that the farmer receives the fruit, rather than that the fruit receives the rain. Some manuscripts modify "brothers" by adding "my" in verse 9, others in verse 10. One substantive change is the substitution of "nobility of character" for "suffering" in verse 10; both words have similar spellings but very different meanings. In verse 11, some manuscripts read "have showed endurance" in the present tense. The most important alternatives occur in verse 11: reading "you have seen" as an imperative, and a substitution of "mercy" for the "purpose" of the Lord. In all of these cases, the NRSV follows the most acceptable readings.

This unit contains three pieces of advice or moral exhortation. The main theme is patience. The root term for endurance *(hypo-monē)* appears in 1:3-4 (as a noun) and 1:12 (in verb form), where it defines one of the major Christian virtues. In this passage it is also used as both a verb and a noun (v. 11). Paired with it, and used only here in James, is the verb *makrothymein* ("to be patient"; in vv. 7 and 8 three times) and its cognate noun "patience" (used once in v. 10). How the two root terms differ in meaning is not clear, although the latter is used for pleading with a superior in the parable in Matt 23:26, 29. It is also used as an attribute of God (in passages such as Rom 2:4; 9:22; 1 Pet 3:20) and of Jesus Christ (1 Tim 3:16). The reference to the Judge in verse 9, then, suggests that Christians are to emulate the patience that God has shown toward them. That suggestion is supported by the final clause in the unit: "the Lord is compassionate and merciful."

A related piece of moral advice is "Do not grumble against one another" (v. 9). At first glance it seems to be out of place here and interrupts the flow of the argument (Dibelius and Greeven 1976, 242, 244). Such a view overlooks two things. First, warnings against the misuse of the tongue have been a theme throughout the letter (e.g., 1:19, 26; 2:12; 3:2, 8-12; 4:11-12). "Grumbling" is not a new concept, but simply one more example of impatience. Those who have no patience are the ones most apt to criticize and condemn others in the community. Second, the rationale for this piece of advice is found in the rest of the same verse. Do not complain so that you will not be judged! It is no great stretch of the imagination to see a parallel in Matt 7:1: "Do not judge, so that you may not be judged." Both sayings see a reciprocal relationship between what we do and what will happen as a result. In other words, verse 9 has a direct link to earlier passages in the letter; and the author fits it into the present context by linking it to the theme of the Judge who is standing at the doors.

The third piece of advice is to "strengthen your hearts" (v. 8). In context, it is not meant as an advertisement for a health fitness program but rather as encouragement for the letter's recipients to rededicate themselves to God. In other words, it has to be read in light of the demand to be single-minded (1:5-6) and to demonstrate the wisdom from above (3:17-18). Such character is the opposite of those who are double-minded (1:6-8; 4:8) and who are friends of the world (4:4).

To support these moral exhortations, James offers a series of five different warrants and examples. The most obvious one is "the coming of the Lord" (vv. 7, 8), which almost certainly coincides with "the Judge . . . standing at the doors" (v. 9; cf. 4:12). The view that Christ will act as God's agent at the final judgment is a consistent element in New Testament eschatology (e.g., Acts 10:42; 17:31; Rom 2:16; 1 Cor 4:5; 2 Tim 4:1, 8; Rev 19:2). Thus, although the referent of "the Lord" is not consistent in James, in this passage it almost certainly refers to the Risen Christ.

The second argument in verse 7 is the example of a farmer. The "farmer" in this case could be a small landowner in danger of losing his property, or it might also refer back to the image of laborers who were defrauded of their wages (v. 4). The reference is so general that it does not help us to locate the audience. In any case, the example uses a quite different experience of a farmer: that of planting the crop and waiting for God's gift of rain to produce a harvest. It is similar to the pericope in Mark 5:26-29, except that there the emphasis falls on an automatic growth that is part of the cycle of nature. Here the emphasis is on rain as the gracious gift of God (cf. 1:17). The mention of early and late rains has frequently been used to locate the recipients of the letter in northern Palestine (Galilee) or western Syria (e.g., Hadidian 1952, 228). The early rains from the Mediterranean occur in the fall (October–November) and soften the ground so that it can be prepared for planting. Winter rains a month or two later benefit those crops. The late rains in the early spring (April–May) mark the end of the harvest and the beginning of the long, dry, summer season. Most commentators agree that this verse is relevant to the situation of James's audience. However, they do not agree on what the "late rains" refer to, and quite correctly there is no consensus on how precisely we can locate the recipients of the letter on the basis of this single verse. The harvest image is linked with judgment at the "Day of the Lord" in Mal 4:1 and with the *parousia* in Rev 14:14-20.

Third, James uses the prophets as an example of people who remained faithful to God even in times of suffering (v. 10). This seems to refer to the Old Testament prophets who spoke in "the name of the Lord." If so, then there has been a sudden shift from verses 8-9. Now "the Lord" seems to refer to God and not to Christ; and that also seems to be the referent of "the Lord" in both occurrences in verse 11. However, we cannot rule out the possibility that Christian prophets are included in the group of those who spoke in the name of God or of Christ and were persecuted, especially in light of the murder of the righteous one in verse 6. There is no strong tradition of the persecution of prophets in the present text of the Old Testament, but it became a prominent theme in the early Christian tradition, perhaps because of their own experience (e.g., Matt 5:12 = Luke 6:23; Matt 23:29-36 = Luke 11:47-51; Matt 23:37 = Luke 13:34; Acts 7:52; Rom 11:3).

The fourth example is that of Job (v. 11). Certainly as we read that book today Job is anything but an exemplar of patience. He refuses to concede to his so-called friends that his suffering is a direct result of his own sin. We as readers know that he was right, since chapters 1-2 tell us that Satan is using Job's suffering in order to test his faithfulness to God; but of course the characters in the story do not know that. Throughout the poetic portion of the book

Job continually rejects the advice of his colleagues, refuses to admit his own guilt, and challenges God to a trial so that he can prove his innocence. The image of Job's patience, which James has probably helped to promote among those who have never read the story of Job carefully, seems to be based on two stages of the tradition: the ancient narrative portion of Job (chaps. 1–2; 42:7-17), in which his fortunes are restored after he has proven his unswerving dedication to God (his "single-mindedness"); and an interpretation of Job in the later Jewish tradition found in the *Testament of Job*. In James, the example of Job is introduced in verse 11 by an emphatic *idou* (RSV = "Behold"; NIV = "As you know"; NRSV = "Indeed") followed by a saying "we call blessed those who showed endurance." This is not cited as a quotation from Scripture, although it has some affinity to Dan 12:12. The saying "But the one who endures to the end will be saved" (Matt 10:22) seems to be a close parallel; but, unlike James, in Matthew the context is a threat of persecution.

The last warrant is an appeal to the "purpose of the Lord" (v. 11). As already noted, "the Lord" here almost certainly refers to God, as it did in the previous verse and as it does in the next clause. The word *telos,* as usual, is ambiguous. It could possibly refer to the "end," that is, to the *parousia.* However, since James views the *parousia* as still in the future, that is an unlikely reading if we accept *eidete* ("you have seen") as the established text. The best alternative is that adopted by the NRSV: "you have seen the purpose of the Lord," namely in the patience shown by the prophets and by Job. It carries a sense of open-endedness that is missing in the NIV translation that you "have seen what the Lord finally brought about." In contrast to 1 Pet 2:21-23, James does not use Jesus' own suffering as an example of endurance.

◊ ◊ ◊ ◊

Throughout this unit we cannot help being struck by three things. First, James places a very high moral demand on his audience. In the face of uncertainty, Christians are to remain patient and to endure. The references to oppression and murder at the hands of the rich, like the earlier reference to being dragged into court (2:6), are so vivid that they suggest more than hypothetical possibilities. Even though the first people to receive this letter may not personally have suffered such trials, they almost certainly knew other Christians who had. They should be prepared to deal with the same experiences in their own lives. Nevertheless, with the exception of the warning not to grumble against one another, all of the other exhortations are positive: be patient; endure; strengthen your hearts. In other words, they should develop and maintain the kind of character that was described in 1:2-4, so that testing leads ultimately toward maturity and completeness.

Second, the unit overflows with reinforcement and encouragement. There is the image of the farmer waiting patiently for the harvest. There is the example of the prophets and of Job. There is the promise that the coming of the Lord is near; the Judge is at the door. There is the promise of blessing for those who endure. Finally, there is a reminder in the final clause that "the Lord is compassionate and merciful." That clause is introduced by *hoti*, which does not appear in most English translations, but which indicates that the character of God undergirds the call for moral perfection.

Finally, even though this unit focuses on personal morality in a time of crisis, it takes place in the context of a Christian community. That is most clear in the warning against grumbling, but it is present in other ways: looking back to the prophets and wise men (personified by Job) of Israel, and looking ahead to the elders of the church (v. 14). For James, the church helps to shape Christian character.

Conduct Within the Community of Faith (5:12-20)

As noted in the introduction to the entire section, this unit has three distinct parts: verse 12 (oath taking); verses 13-18 (prayer); and verses 19-20 (reclaiming those who have left the community). The middle piece actually combines subordinate themes (illness, the forgiveness of sins) with the dominant theme of prayer. We will examine these in the exegetical analysis.

Stylistically, several things stand out. The unit is introduced by *pro panton de* ("above all"), which seems to have two functions.

It is sometimes used to emphasize the last in a series, but here it indicates that a new unit or new theme is about to begin. Even more important, it tells the reader that we are approaching the end of the letter. In Paul's letters this transition is usually accomplished with the word *finally (loipon* or *to loipon:* e.g., 2 Cor 13:11; Phil 3:1 and again in 4:8; 1 Thess 4:1; 2 Thess 3:1). The "above all" construction is also found in 1 Pet 3:8, where it has a different function, and in *Did.* 10:4 in a eucharistic setting. The word *kai* ("and") appears nine times in verses 15-18, plus once in a contraction *(kan),* but these tend to disappear in translation. Three different words for prayer are used: the usual term *proseuchomai* and cognates (vv. 13, 14, 17, 18); a shorter form of the noun *euchē* (v. 15) and the verb *euchomai* (a preferred form in v. 16); and *deēsis* (v. 16). In verses 19-20, the words "wander" and "bring back" are each repeated for the sake of emphasis. The repetition of "brothers" in verses 12 and 19 has already been noted.

Textual variants are not very important in this unit. In verse 12, *logos* is inserted in some manscripts to read "Let your word be. . . ." This is almost certainly an assimilation to Matt 5:37. A few omit the duplication of "Yes" and "No" in verse 12, and others substitute "Lest you fall into hypocrisy" for "Lest you fall under judgment" (NRSV: "so that you may not fall under condemnation"). In verse 14, some texts insert "him" after "anointing," and some omit "of the Lord" after the name. Word substitutions occur in verse 16 ("transgressions" for "sins," and a different word for "prayer"). Some insert "the way of" before "truth" in verse 19. One change that does affect the meaning in verse 20 is to read "let him know," as a number of commentators do, instead of the second person "you should know" (NRSV; cf. NIV: "remember this"). Finally, a few manuscripts could not resist adding an "Amen" at the end of the letter.

◊ ◊ ◊ ◊

Oaths: Controlling One's Speech (5:12)

Controlling one's speech can be viewed simply as a matter of personal morality. From that perspective, whether or not to take an oath would be a purely private matter. However, James does not view it in that way. He lived in a world in which speech was the fundamental means of interpersonal communication. For him, every speech act must be evaluated in terms of its effect on someone else. On the negative side, we have seen his warnings: be slow to speak (1:19); bridle your tongues (1:26; 3:2); avoid cursing another human being (3:9-10); do not boast or be false to the truth (3:14); do not speak evil against one another (4:11-12); do not boast (4:16); do not grumble (5:9). Making no errors in speech leads to perfection (3:2); and yet James's view of the tongue is decidedly negative (3:5b-12). It is only in the rest of the present unit that he gives us a positive view of the role that speech can play within the community of faith, particularly in prayer.

In the Jewish tradition oaths were permitted. What was prohibited was to misuse God's name (Exod 20:7 = Deut 5:11), in other words to swear falsely. Leviticus 19:12, in close proximity to the love commandment, reads: "You shall not swear falsely by my name, profaning the name of your God" (Johnson 1982, 397-98 on the use of this passage in James). Similar warnings are found in Zech 5:3-5 and Mal 3:5 and in the later Jewish tradition: "Do not accustom your mouth to oaths, nor habitually utter the name of the Holy One" (Sir 23:9). The thrust of these passages is to avoid the colloquial use of phrases such as "I swear to God" or "As God is my witness."

James 5:12 has to be understood not only against that background, and also in conjunction with Matt 5:33-37 (one of the six antitheses in the Sermon on the Mount) and a third form of the saying in Justin Martyr's *1 Apol.* 1.16.5. The saying in James is shorter and less elaborate. That may indicate his version is earlier, although that it is not necessarily the case (Betz 1995, 266-67). In James, the saying is in four parts. It begins with an absolute prohibition in the present tense, suggesting a current situation: "Do not *(mē)* swear." That is followed by a set of three stipulations, each introduced by "neither" (*mēte,* even though that is not clear in the translation): by heaven, by earth, or by any other oath. The third stage is a positive injunction: "Let your 'Yes' be yes and your 'No' be no." The final step provides a rationale for the prohibition: "so that you may not fall under condemnation." Literally it reads "under judgment," a phrase that appears nowhere else in the New Testament. It is consistent with previous warnings against judging, which we have seen in James (2:12-13; 4:11-12; and 5:9). The Matthean version differs in several respects. In the opening charge the verb "swear" is in the aorist tense and is modified by the adverb "at all." In the second part, Matthew has the same first two stipulations but expands them ("either by heaven, for it is the throne of God, or by the earth, for it is his footstool"). Then, in place of "any other oath" he adds two different stipulations: "or by Jerusalem, for it is the city of the great King. And do not swear by your head, for you cannot make one hair white or black." The third stage is slightly different, with the addition of the word *logos:* "Let your word be 'Yes, Yes' or 'No, No.'" Finally, instead of the appeal to judgment, the conclusion is "anything more than this comes from the evil one." In either form of the tradition there is an obvious radicalizing of the prohibition against oaths. Most commentators, however, tend to agree with the position stated by Peter Davids (1982, 190): "James, then, prohibits not official oaths, such as in courts . . . but the use of oaths in everyday discourse to prove integrity."

Prayer, Illness, and Forgiveness of Sins (5:13-18)

These verses all deal with the same theme (prayer) but approach it in several different ways. The theme is introduced (vv. 13-14) by a series of three questions about the anonymous "anyone" *(tis);* each is answered abruptly with a recommended course of action. This is another example of the diatribe style. In the NRSV the questions are transposed into the second-person plural, and in the Jerusalem Bible they are interpreted as hypothetical questions ("If any one . . ."). The most literal translation of verses 13-14 is that of the RSV:

> Is anyone among you suffering? Let him pray. Is any cheerful? Let him sing praise. Is any among you sick? Let him call for the elders of the church . . .

The phrase "among you" in the first and third of those questions establishes a more intimate relationship between the author and his audience. It also shows that prayer is a communal and not just a personal concern. "Suffering" in this case does not mean sickness. Rather, it implies adversity of some kind, probably the kind of discrimination and harassment suffered by members of a new, unpopular religious movement. Like the "trials" mentioned in 1:2, James refuses to give the term any specific content. The term links their situation to the suffering of the prophets in verse 10, where the same word was used. To be "cheerful" implies a sense of contentment and general well-being; that mood should be an occasion for singing. The word for singing is *psalletō,* from the same stem as "psalms" and "to sing psalms," as in Pss 7:17 ("I will . . . sing praise to the name of the LORD, the Most High") and 9:11 ("Sing praises to the LORD, who dwells in Zion"). We know that psalms were used in the worship of the early church (e.g., Col 3:16 = Eph 5:19; cf. 1 Cor 14:15), so this is an invitation not just to hum around the house but to participate in corporate worship.

The third question involves a subtheme, that of illness. The verb implies weakness, not a terminal illness. It assumes that the person is well enough to call for (literally "summon") help. On the role of the "elders" in the "church," both mentioned only in this verse in James, see the introduction. From the description given here, the elders play a pastoral role of caring for the sick; other duties are unspecified. Also, in light of verse 16 where congregants are urged to pray for one another, it is clear that elders act as representatives of the entire congregation. The actions of the elders involve four things: prayer; anointing the head of the sick person with (olive) oil; using the name of the Lord, probably spoken aloud. All of these actions are mentioned in verse 14. The fourth item is their faith (v. 15), which leads into another topic or subtheme.

In addition to its many practical uses, oil was often used in the Near East for a variety of other reasons. In the familiar Ps 23:5, "you anoint my head with oil" is a symbol that celebrates the grace of God (cf. Ps 133:2; Eccl 9:8). The anointing of Jesus' feet in Luke 7:36-50 is a mark of hospitality and homage; note verse 46 ("You did not anoint my head with oil, but she has anointed my feet with ointment"). In Matt 6:17, anointing the head with oil is linked to fasting, thus giving it a ceremonial meaning. Medicinal uses of oil are also found in Isa 1:6 and in other sources such as *J. W.* 1.657 (Herod's bath in hot oil). Mark 6:13 summarizes a practice that was apparently common among early Christian missionaries: "They cast out many demons, and anointed with oil many who were sick and cured them." In James there is no suggestion that he is describing an exorcism (*contra* Dibelius and Greeven 1976, 252), nor is the oil seen as a magical potion. Rather, the oil seems to celebrate the power of God to heal.

That, of course, leaves open the question of whether "in the name of the Lord" refers to God or to Christ. We have seen both references in the previous unit. In this case, it seems more likely that James conforms to the practice of the early church, particularly according to Luke, which is to pray for healing in the name of Jesus Christ (Mark 9:38 and Luke 10:17 = exorcisms; Acts 3:6; 4:10; cf. Acts 9:34 = healings). It is not possible to isolate any one of the four elements (prayer, oil, name, faith) and say that it is *the* factor that is responsible for the cure, since the healing is ultimately in God's hands.

However, James does add that faith has a role: "The prayer of faith will save the sick, and the Lord will raise them up" (v. 15). The synoptic Gospels often report that Jesus healed in response to a person's faith (Mark 5:34 = Matt 9:27 = Luke 8:48; Mark 10:50 = Luke 18:42; Matt 15:28; Luke 7:50; 17:19); and Mark 2:5 pictures Jesus healing a paralytic in response to the faith of his friends. Another striking parallel appears in Acts 3:16 when Peter explains the healing of a cripple in the following words: "And by faith in his name (i.e., referring back to Jesus Christ in 3:6), his name itself has made this man strong, whom you see and know; and the faith that is through Jesus has given him this perfect health in the presence of all of you." In James the promises that the prayer of faith "will save the sick" and that "the Lord will raise them up" (v. 15) are sometimes understood to refer to eternal salvation and to the resurrection, in which case "the Lord" would have to refer to God. According to that view, the person being prayed for is terminally ill, so that there is no hope except life after death. That text was the exegetical basis for defending the sacrament of Extreme Unction by Roman Catholics and for refuting it by Protestants. As noted judiciously by Luke Timothy Johnson (1995b, 342) "the main effect of this preoccupation has been to distort the text and require it to address issues beyond its scope." Quite apart from that issue, verses 13-15 seem to be driven by the expectation that the sick person will recover. "Saved" in this context means "will get well," just as "the Lord will raise them up" (with Christ as the presumed agent) implies that they will be healed.

In addition to *faith,* verses 15-16 introduce *sin* as a second subtheme. In the Jewish tradition, sickness was often seen as a result of sin. That was the position of Job's friends. In order to be cured, then, sins would have to be forgiven. That occurs in the dramatic story of the healing of the paralytic in Mark 2:5 with Jesus' words "Son, your sins are forgiven" followed later in the same incident with "I say to you, . . . take your mat and go to your home" (2:11). In James 5:15, the link between forgiveness of sins and healing is less obvious, but it is still present. When the mention of sins is introduced, it still applies to the sick person. Not only will the person be saved and be raised up, but sins that the person has committed will be forgiven. According to this sequence, healing is not contingent on the forgiveness of sins, as it seems to be in Mark. However, in verse 16, there is a sudden shift from the hypothetical "any among you." James now addresses them directly: "Therefore confess your sins to one another, and pray for one another, so that you may be healed." The shift from third to second person, and the fact that prayer is now a mutual act rather than one performed by the elders, may mean that this verse originally existed in some other context; but our task is to try to understand it in its present context.

Three comments are in order. First, the connection between sin and healing is left unclear. The readers/hearers of the letter are to confess their sins, and they are to pray, but we cannot be sure whether the healing is a result of one or both of those actions. In any case, the healing belongs to the Lord; it is not something that they can manipulate. Second, they are to confess their sins within the community of faith. Of course, they can pray directly to God for forgiveness, but that is not the point here. James does not say how such confession is to be done, whether privately or publicly; but it is obviously an important element in their communal life. Earlier, members of the community were urged to establish mutual trust by refusing to take oaths (v. 12). Now they must maintain that trust by admitting their mistakes, presumably including mistakes in speaking (3:2). Third, they are told to pray not for themselves but for one another. A major function of prayer, as a form of Christian speech, is to foster mutual encouragement and support. It is just the opposite of the sniping and backbiting that James attacked in 3:9-10 and 4:11. Verse 16 ends with a summary observation, which is difficult to translate. A literal translation might be that the prayer of a righteous person "works with a great deal of power" or (as in the RSV) "has great power in its effects." The phrase "powerful and effective" adopted by both the NRSV and the NIV carries the same general sense. As in verse 6, we have to decide whether "the righteous" refers to an individual or to anyone whose character and lifestyle reflects the purpose of the Lord (v. 11). Almost everything in this unit points toward the more generic interpretation.

Just as Job was used as an example of patience, so Elijah is now introduced as a model of effective prayer (vv. 17-18). In fact, Elijah is presented as a man who is a "fellow sufferer with us" *(homoiopathēs)*. The example is presented as though it is a simple paraphrase of the Old Testament story (1 Kgs 17:1–2 Kgs 2:12), but there are several curious things to note about James's use of it. First, even though we have several examples of Elijah's powerful prayers, the Old Testament never reports that he prayed for God to create a drought, as James suggests (v. 17). Second, James says that the drought lasted for three and a half years, a detail not mentioned in the Old Testament. Finally, James focuses on Elijah's ability to bring rain for the harvest (v. 18). Thus the example of Elijah illustrates not just the power of prayer, but also the grace of God in delivering rain. It reinforces the agricultural image of the expectant farmer at the beginning of the previous unit

(vv. 7-8). It also reminds us of the very different kind of harvest in 3:17-18.

Rescuing Backsliders (5:19-20)

The letter concludes in a rather surprising way, with an issue that has not been mentioned before, at least directly. James encourages the letter's readers to bring back into the community those Christians who have left. Nothing tells us whether they left for doctrinal reasons (and were therefore apostates), for disagreements over moral issues such as treatment of the poor, or simply for other personal reasons. These verses begin with the usual "brothers" and the familiar "anyone among you," although this time (in contrast to v. 13) the verb is in the subjunctive and is introduced by "if" *(ean)*. The metaphor is that of a person who has wandered away and become lost, but who needs someone to go to the rescue. The wandering is from "the truth" (v. 19; cf. 3:14) or from "the error of his way" (v. 20 RSV; cf. "his error" NIV). The challenge is to bring back such a person (vv. 19, 20), a reminder of the image of "returning" used frequently by the Old Testament prophets to call the people of Israel to reaffirm their responsibility to God (e.g., Isa 55:7; Jer 4:1; Hos 6:1). In the Gospels the same term appears primarily in the context of Scripture citations (Matt 13:15 = Isa 6:10; Luke 1:16-17, a reference to Elijah) and the prediction of Peter's betrayal (Luke 22:32). In Acts (3:19; 9:35; 11:21) and in Paul's letters (1 Thess 1:9; 2 Cor 3:16), it becomes basically a technical term for conversion. For James, however, the project is not missionary activity to gain new converts but a rescue operation, whose goal is to bring back those who have left the community. The most difficult decision for the translator is to decide who benefits from the rescue. The clause is "will save his soul from death"; but whose soul? That of the saver or the saved, the rescuer or the rescued? Nothing in the text itself helps us to make that decision. However, the total context of this unit clearly suggests that the person who has been persistent in prayer and who has been willing to confess sins does not need to "cover a multitude of sins." That phrase may be drawn loosely from Prov 10:12, but it is cited as "love covers a multitude of sins" in 1 Pet 4:8 and *1 Clem.* 49.5. The recipient of the benefit, then, is not the rescuer but the sinner. Not only is that person's soul saved from death, but equally as important, that person once again becomes a functioning and contributing member of the community of faith.

◊ ◊ ◊ ◊

From a modern perspective, this last section—particularly the last unit—seems like an anticlimax. Rather than building to a dramatic review of the major themes of the Christian moral life (as in 4:7-10), James seems to run out of steam and deals with practical issues that should have been dealt with earlier in the letter. There are many different ways to explain such an inconclusive conclusion; but, like the earliest ending of Mark's Gospel, it is all we have.

However, we at least have to wrestle with the possibility that the issues in this section were the ones the author really wanted to discuss in a personal, pastoral mode before signing off. How and why should Christians be patient during a time when they were being treated unfairly and unjustly by the rich and powerful? If some members of the community were being oppressed or were ill, how should they seek support, not only from elders who were "official" representatives of the local community, but also from others? If some other recipients of the letter could not find a way to deal with their feelings of sin and guilt, how could they discover a positive way to find forgiveness? If others had left the community, for whatever reason, was there any possibility of bringing them back? The final section of the letter, then, falls under the heading of what used to be called "practical theology." Like much of the letter as a whole, its pragmatic spirit may be its greatest appeal.

Luther may have denigrated the letter because he thought its theology was inferior to the Pauline doctrine of justification and because its Christology was not fully developed. What he failed to realize is the appeal that James has precisely because it does not get entangled in great theological debates. In the tradition of Jewish and hellenistic wisdom, James grapples with personal issues such as temptation, prayer, proper speech, controlling one's temper, and so forth. More than any other New Testament document, it focuses on how to develop a Christian character and a Christian lifestyle in the face of a hostile world (one that not only sees no need for God, but which is in fact opposed to God).

SELECT BIBLIOGRAPHY

WORKS CITED IN THE TEXT
(EXCLUDING COMMENTARIES)

Adamson, James B. 1989. *James: The Man and His Message.* Grand Rapids, MI: Eerdmans.

Baasland, E. 1988. "Literarische Form, Thematik und geschichtliche Einordnung des Jakobusbriefes." ANRW II, 25.2:3659-62.

Baker, William R. 1995. *Personal Speech-Ethics in the Epistle of James.* WUNT 2.68. Tübingen: Mohr-Siebeck.

Bauckham, Richard. 1990. *Jude and the Relatives of Jesus in the Early Church.* Edinburgh: T. & T. Clark.

Betz, Hans Dieter. 1995. *The Sermon on the Mount.* Hermeneia. Minneapolis: Fortress.

Braumann, Georg. 1962. "Der theologische Hintergrund des Jakobusbriefes." *TZ* 18:401-10.

Brown, William P. 1996. *Character in Crisis.* Grand Rapids, MI: Eerdmans.

Cargal, Timothy B. 1993. *Restoring the Diaspora: Discursive Structure and Purpose in the Epistle of James.* SBLDS 144. Atlanta: Scholars Press.

Countryman, L. William. 1988. *Dirt, Greed & Sex.* Philadelphia: Fortress.

Douglas, Mary. 1966. *Purity and Danger.* London: Routledge & Kegan Paul.

Elliott, John H. 1981. *A Home for the Homeless.* Philadelphia: Fortress.

Felder, Cain H. 1982. "Wisdom, Law and Social Concern in the Epistle of James." Ph.D. diss., Columbia University.

Feuillet, André. 1964. "Le sense du mot parousie dans l'evagile de Matthieu: comparaison entre Matth XXIV et Jac V, 1-11." In *The Background of the New Testament and Its Eschatology,* edited by W. D. Davies and D. Daube. Cambridge: Cambridge University Press, 261-80.

Francis, Fred O. 1970. "The Form and Function of the Opening and Closing Paragraphs of James and John." *ZNW* 61:110-26.

Freyne, Sean. 1980. *Galilee from Alexander the Great to Hadrian, 323 B.C.E. to 135 C.E.* Wilmington, DE: Michael Glazier.

Furnish, Victor Paul. 1972. *The Love Command in the New Testament.* Nashville: Abingdon.

Hadidian, D. Y. 1952. "Palestinian Pictures in the Epistle of James." *ExpTim* 63:227-28.

Hanks, Thomas D. 1992. "Poor, Poverty: New Testament." *ABD* 5:414-24. New York: Doubleday.

———. 1983. *God So Loved the Third World.* Translated by James C. Decker. Maryknoll, NY: Orbis.

Hartin, Patrick J. 1991. *James and the Q Sayings of Jesus.* JSNTSup 47. Sheffield: JSOT.

Hays, Richard B. 1996. *The Moral Vision of the New Testament.* San Francisco: HarperSanFrancisco.

Horsley, Richard. 1989a. *Sociology and the Jesus Movement.* New York: Crossroad.

———. 1989b. "Questions About Redactional Strata and the Social Relations Reflected in Q." SBLSP:186-203.

———. 1995. *Galilee: History, Politics, People.* Valley Forge, PA: Trinity Press International.

Johnson, Luke T. 1982. "The Use of Leviticus 19 in the Letter of James." *JBL* 101/3:301-401.

———. 1983. "James 3:13–4:10 and the *Topos* PERI PHTHONOU." *NovT* 25:327-47.

———. 1995a. "The Social World of James: Literary Analysis and Historical Reconstruction." In *The Social World of the First Christians,* edited by L. M. White and O. L. Yarbrough. Minneapolis: Fortress, 178-97.

Keck, Leander E. 1966. "The Poor Among the Saints in Jewish Christianity and Qumran." *ZNW* 57:54-78.

Kelly, Francis X. 1973. "Poor and Rich in the Epistle of James." Ph.D. diss., Temple University.

Maynard-Reid, Pedrito U. 1987. *Poverty and Wealth in James.* Maryknoll, NY: Orbis.

Meeks, Wayne A. 1974. "The Image of the Androgyne: Some Uses of a Symbol in Earliest Christianity." *HR* 13:165-208.

Penner, Todd C. 1996. *The Epistle of James and Eschatology.* JSNTSup 121. Sheffield: Sheffield Academic Press.

Perdue, Leo. 1981. "Paraenesis and the Epistle of James." *ZNW* 72:241-56.

Perkins, Pheme. 1982. "James 3:16–4:3." *Int* 36:283-87. Louisville: Westminster/John Knox.

Pleins, J. David. 1992. *Poor, Poverty: Old Testament. ABD* "5:402-14."

Selwyn, Edward Gordon. 1958. *The First Epistle of St. Peter*. London: Macmillan.

Sleeper, C. Freeman. 1992. *The Bible and the Moral Life*. Louisville: Westminster/John Knox.

———. 1996. *The Victorious Christ*. Louisville: Westminster/John Knox.

Tamez, Elsa. 1990. *The Scandalous Message of James: Faith Without Works Is Dead*. Translated by John Eagleson. New York: Crossroad.

Via, Dan Ott, Jr. 1969. "The Right Strawy Epistle Reconsidered: A Study in Biblical Ethics and Hermeneutic." *JR* 49:253-67.

Ward, Roy Bowen. 1966. "The Communal Concern of the Epistle of James." Ph.D. diss., Harvard University.

———. 1968. "The Works of Abraham." *HTR* 61:283-90.

———. 1969. "Partiality in the Assembly: James 2:2-4." *HTR* 62:87-97.

Wessel, W. W. 1982. "James, Epistle of," in *ISBE,* ed. Geoffrey W. Bromiley. Grand Rapids, MI: Eerdmans, 2:959-66.

COMMENTARIES (BOTH CITED AND NOT CITED)

Davids, Peter H. 1982. *The Epistle of James: A Commentary on the Greek Text*. NIGTC. Grand Rapids, MI: Eerdmans. Reaches conservative conclusions regarding authorship (James the Lord's brother) and provenance (Palestine before the Jewish War) in open dialogue with other viewpoints. Knowledge of Greek useful.

Dibelius, Martin, and Heinrich Greeven. 1976. *James: A Commentary on the Epistle of James*. Translated by Michael A. Williams. Hermeneia. Philadelphia: Fortress. The original commentary by Dibelius, which appeared in 1921 and was revised by Greeven in 1964, has shaped all subsequent discussions of the letter. The composition was post-Pauline and anonymous. Since the genre is parenesis, the letter contains no consistent theology.

Johnson, Luke Timothy. 1995b. *The Letter of James*. AB. New York: Doubleday. Sets a new standard with encyclopedic references to ancient and modern sources. Challenges Dibelius's position at many points including authorship, date of composition, and genre.

Laws, Sophie. 1980. *The Epistle of James*. HNTC. New York: Harper & Row. Her arguments reflect those of Dibelius in most respects. She locates James and his audience within hellenized Judaism and the early Christian mission to Gentiles ("God-fearers").

Martin, Ralph P. 1988. *James*. *WBC*. Waco, TX: Word. Extensive introduction, notes, and bibliography. Comments on the Greek text are accessible to those without knowledge of Greek. Argues that an original letter of James was later revised by a disciple in Antioch.

Mayor, J. B. 1892. *The Epistle of St. James*. London: Macmillan. Despite its age, the introduction and notes are still valuable. Contains extensive quotations from ancient sources in the original languages, knowledge of which is presupposed.

Mussner, Franz. 1964. *Der Jakobusbrief*. HKNT 13.1. Freiburg: Herder. *Contra* Dibelius, accepts as authentic the salutation, namely that James wrote this letter to Jewish Christians in the Diaspora about 60 CE, although a secretary may be responsible for the excellent Greek.

Perkins, Pheme. 1995. *First and Second Peter, James, and Jude*. IBC:83-140. Louisville: Westminster/John Knox. A valuable, highly readable analysis from a modern literary point of view. Interprets the letter in the context of hellenistic-Jewish documents.

Reicke, Bo. 1964. *The Epistles of James, Peter, and Jude*. AB 1-66. Garden City, NY: Doubleday. Argues that James is an anonymous circular letter encouraging Christians who faced persecution during the reign of Domitian (c. 90 CE), and warning them not to engage in riots or other zealotic activity.

Ropes, James Hardy. 1916. *A Critical and Exegetical Commentary on the Epistle of St. James*. ICC. Edinburgh: T & T Clark. Reprint, 1978. Outdated by more recent historical, sociological, and rhetorical studies, but raises questions still worth considering.

Vouga, François. 1984. *L'Épitre de Saint Jacques*. CNT 2.13a. Geneva: Labor et Fides. The letter was written to Jewish Christians by an anonymous author at the end of the first Christian century.

Wall, Robert W. 1997. *Community of the Wise*. Valley Forge, PA: Trinity Press International. Reads James within the context of the biblical canon as an alternative to Paul. Emphasizes true religion as a concern for the suffering poor, reinforced by eschatological motifs.

INDEX

Abraham, 16, 77, 81-83, 107, 112
Antioch, 32, 37, 40
apocalyptic. *See* eschatology.

brother(s), 16, 20, 53-54, 60, 67, 68, 71, 77, 85, 115, 130, 144

character, 42-43, 48-50, 63-65, 95, 116
church, 34, 69, 87-88
Clement *(1 Clement)*, 27, 29-30, 51, 81, 83, 109, 112-13, 115, 120
communication, 17, 48, 60-63
conflict, 96-99, 102-9

demonic powers (devil), 42, 100, 111-12
Diaspora. *See* Dispersion.
diatribe, 16-18, 79, 139
discipline, 61, 65, 67, 86-89
Dispersion, 17, 31-33, 45-47, 103
double-minded (doubters), 43, 50-52, 57, 106, 112

elders, 34, 136, 139-40
Elijah, 16, 143-44
endurance (patience), 49, 52, 132, 135-36
eschatology, 23, 54, 56, 112, 120, 123-24, 127, 129-30
 parousia, 23, 130-31, 133
ethics (morality), 22, 42-43, 60, 63, 109-16

faith, 49, 51-53, 71-72, 77-78, 106
 and works, 79-84
favoritism (partiality), 67-72, 75, 77
friendship, 87, 92, 107

God, 41-42, 51, 56-59, 66, 71, 93-94, 102, 108-9, 134

healing, 139-44
humility, 53, 62, 98, 109, 113-14, 120

James
 in Acts, 31, 36-37

authorship, 25, 39-41, 45-46
 identity, 34-39, 87, 128
Jesus, 34, 41, 47, 68
Job, 16, 134-35
joy, 48-49
judge (judgment), 23, 70-71, 88, 116, 133

law, 22, 57, 64-65, 68, 73-76, 114-16
Luke, 24-25, 71
Luther, Martin, 25, 145

Matthew, 24-25, 32, 56, 63-64, 71, 73, 75-76, 98, 105, 121, 133, 135, 138-39
morality. *See* ethics.

parenesis, 18-19, 47
partiality. *See* favoritism.
Paul
 letters by, 17-18, 33, 87, 137
 theology of, 25-26, 53, 58-59, 72, 74, 78, 81-83, 88, 99
perfection, 49-50, 89
Peter (1 Peter), 17, 26-28, 31, 46-47, 98, 111-12
poor (poverty), 32-33, 53-54, 66, 70-72, 76-79, 125-28
prayer, 51-52, 106, 137, 139-44
prophecy (prophets), 22, 117, 121, 127, 134

"Q," 24-25, 32, 33-34, 123
Qumran, 23, 33, 79, 98, 108

Rahab, 16, 77, 83-84
religion, 65-67, 92
rich, 53-54, 70-72, 124
 See also wealth.

self-control. *See* discipline.
Septuagint (LXX), 23, 74, 83, 106, 109, 123
speech, 84-86, 89-95
 cursing, 93-94, 99
 oaths, 130, 137-39
 slander, 115

151